Praise for *Collaborative Intelligence*

Collaboration has been the elephant and we the blind men—all touching parts and thinking ... ɔorative *Intelligence*, we finally have the whole elephant! In a comprehensive and compelling way, Marianc ... ιe many facets of collaboration, including both the obvious (communication and trust) and the less than oḃ ... n safety, measurement, and mode). In doing so, they create a must-read for any leader aiming to harness the puῳɕ. ᴢ
—Jeanne Liedtka, Professor at UVA Darden School of Business and author of *Experiencing Design*

Collaboration involves an intelligence ... a stewardship of time, space, visualization, methods, and connection. It is an accessible craft, but we need guides and mentors. In this regard, Jim and Mariano are an inspiration.
—Sunni Brown, social entrepreneur, bestselling author, Founding Gamestormer

Collaborative Intelligence is really about intentional intelligent collaboration. That requires leaders and managers who recognize that working well together is not enough—people need tools and frameworks to bring out the best in each other. That's why there's this book.
—Michael Schrage, Research Fellow, MIT Sloan School Initiative on the Digital Economy
and author of *Shared Minds: The New Technologies of Collaboration*

Execs and leaders who understand the importance of employee experience and the outcomes unlocked through meaningful collaboration will undoubtedly find new possibilities in *Collaborative Intelligence*. For those skeptical leaders, the future of your business demands that you set aside your judgment and pick up this book.
—Douglas Ferguson, President of Voltage Control and author of *Magical Meetings*

Team collaboration has always been the difference between success and failure. In a world where 90% of our collaboration is now digital, designing and creating new methods of virtual collaboration has become our highest priority. *Collaborative Intelligence* explains exactly how to do that and it's a must-read for every entrepreneur and executive wanting to innovate and change the world.
—Al Ramadan, Founder and CEO of Play Bigger

This engaging, accessible playbook provides a bevy of thoughtful models and templates to bring needed rigor to the critical work of collaboration design. Honoring the dynamics of the modern workplace, *Collaborative Intelligence* equips all teams—whether synchronous or asynchronous, in-person or remote—with the tools they need to be truly collaborGREAT.
—Deb Mashek, PhD, author of *Collabor(h)ate: How to Build Incredible Collaborative
Relationships at Work (Even If You'd Rather Work Alone)*

Mariano and Jim have put together a seminal work on what it means to truly collaborate. They draw upon their vast knowledge of living in this space for years and have synthesized it into compelling visuals for the reader to easily understand.

—David J. Bland, Founder and CEO of Precoil

The timing of this book couldn't be more perfect. Never before have so many factors challenged effective collaboration. Mariano and Jim take an honest and critical look at the state of collaboration and leave you with a playbook for success today and tomorrow!

—Joe Lalley, Founder of Joe Lalley Experience Design

To stay relevant in this era of change, leaders need to redesign how we work together, not return back to how things used to be. *Collaborative Intelligence* is a dynamic, engaging, and extremely valuable blueprint for those who are looking to build cultures of innovation. This is a must-read for all leaders who are looking to unlock the genius of their teams.

—Sheela Subramanian, Vice President of Slack's Future Forum and author of *How the Future Works*

Our favorite saying at XPLANE is that "The smartest person in the room is the room." Time and time again we see that the most evolutionary and revolutionary innovations come from great collaborative teams. If you also believe this to be true, *Collaborative Intelligence* should be your playbook to unlock the power of the diverse teams around you.

—Aric Wood, CEO of XPLANE and author of *The Strategy Activation Playbook*

Collaborative Intelligence distills a universe of valuable thinking and resources into a concise, accessible, practical guide for organizations to tap the extraordinary collective potential of their people. Highly recommended!

—Ross Dawson, futurist, keynote speaker, and bestselling author of five books, including *Thriving on Overload*

Collaborative Intelligence makes the much-needed business case for investment in the mindset of collaboration. An irresistible read, infused with inimitable riffs from adjacent models of collaboration, including my personal teaching favorite, lessons from the jazz ensemble.

—Rebecca Robins, educator, author, Global Chief Learning and Culture Officer at Interbrand

COLLABORATIVE

INTELLIGENCE

COLLABORATIVE INTELLIGENCE

Mariano Battan **Jim Kalbach**

The New Way to Bring Out the
Genius, Fun, and Productivity
in Any Team

WILEY

Published by John Wiley & Sons, Inc., Hoboken, New Jersey.
Published simultaneously in Canada.

For general information on our other products and services or for technical support, please contact our Customer Care Department within the United States at (800) 762-2974, outside the United States at (317) 572-3993 or fax (317) 572-4002.

Wiley also publishes its books in a variety of electronic formats. Some content that appears in print may not be available in electronic formats. For more information about Wiley products, visit our web site at www.wiley.com.

Library of Congress Cataloging-in-Publication Data is Available:
ISBN: 9781119896036 (cloth)
ISBN: 9781119896548 (ePub)
ISBN: 9781119896555 (ePDF)

Cover Design: XPLANE

SKY10042023_022423

To future generations of collaboration designers.

Contents

Chapter 1

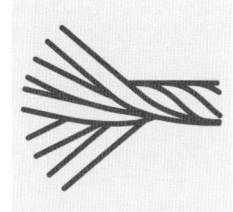

Collaboration in Principle   1

Connecting the Genius of Your Teams

- Beyond Meeting Hygiene
- Collaborate Smarter
- Principles of Collaboration
- Welcome to the Renaissance of Teamwork

Chapter 2

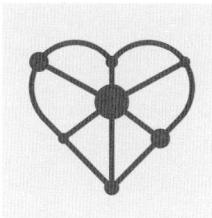

Relational Intelligence   19

The Human Aspect of Collaboration

- Trust Falls Won't Solve Your Problems
- The Collaboration Mindset
- Team Needs
- Relationship Goals

Chapter 3

Collaboration Design   35

Making the Collaboration Experience Deliberate

- Who Can Fix Bad Meetings?
- What Does a Collaboration Designer Do?
- How Can You Make Collaboration Work Better?
- Declaration of Interdependence
- Understanding the Collaboration Experience
- Modeling Collaboration Experiences

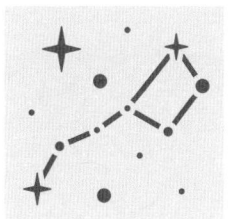
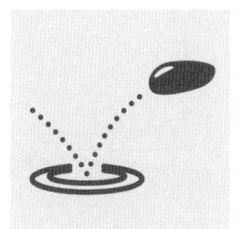

Innovating
Is Collaborating

The CFO of a unicorn EdTech company recently shared a story with us. He explained that while his organization kept going during the COVID-19 pandemic, he noticed something surprising: Individual productivity actually went up, yet when it came to strategizing and solving complex problems as a team, it was clear that something was missing. Team productivity had gone down.

It was difficult for groups to find the time to come together for complex problem-solving. A general lack of alignment caused re-work, delayed schedules, among other things, and set teams back. Teams also struggled to build consensus and confidence.

They of course tried adding more tools to the toolbox, but that didn't completely fix things. Seeing this negative impact, the immediate answer was to go back to the office.

We hear this from our customers all the time. Go back to the office. Go back to the water cooler. That font of innovation that seems to create ideas—or at least that's what we think because that one time we had that great idea there, the one that transformed our company. But was it really like that? Or was it just a place for people to talk and gossip?

When it comes to innovation, we can do better. We must.

It's no secret that organizations today struggle to harness the power of innovation. Evidence suggests that CEOs want a more cutting-edge culture and more agile teams. They're seeking the fountain of youth for their organizations, yet real innovation remains difficult to achieve.

Many organizations strive to make innovation a process. Models and methods for innovation abound. Some describe it using a stage-gate model. Others look at innovation as a cycle with loops and phases. Still others distinguish between types of innovation—as in Doblin's 10 types of innovation—noting that each has its own unique dynamics.

From another point of view, innovation is seen as something that's fueled by luck, something that can't be controlled or managed. For instance, the now-infamous story of the Post-it® developed at 3M is held up as a chance event. The company was trying to make a super-strong adhesive and ended up with a solution that led to the invention.

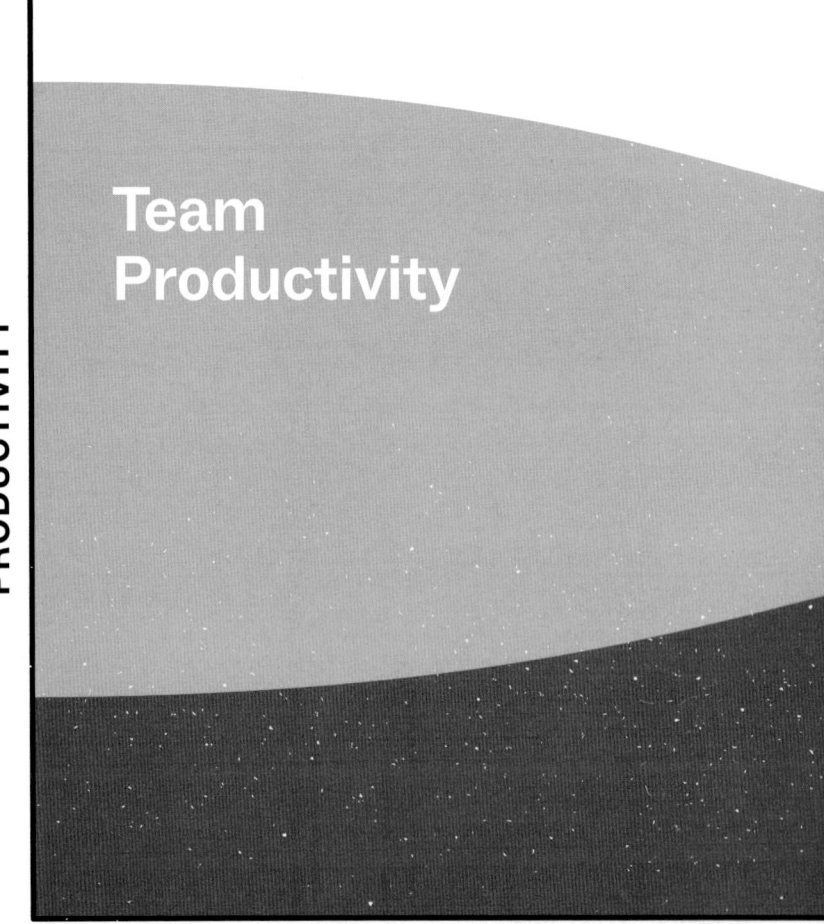

Individual Productivity

(Spoiler alert: It wasn't luck—the sticky note was a direct byproduct of having the right collaborative environment.)

But eureka is not on tap at the water cooler. Serendipity won't be found at the Ping Pong table. Aha doesn't roam the hallways. And when what works in theory doesn't work in practice, what then?

The truth is that innovation is neither formula nor accident: It's people and collaboration.

Innovation is what happens when teams work together solving real problems, improving products and services, and driving business outcomes. It's teams doing the hard work—trusting, playing, prototyping, and producing. Innovation is the team turning possibility into reality, working together to imagine a better future and doing what's necessary to make it happen.

It's not some lone genius, nor is it only a few teams in the labs. Innovation is the responsibility of all teams in all departments and across all business workflows.

Rather than building momentum, teams are more often worn down by a web of endless meetings. Trapped in a room or a Zoom, there's too much talk and too little understanding. In some meetings, a lack of structure leads to chaos. In others, the well-planned agenda leaves no space for questions, exploration, or innovative ideas.

The harsh reality of work today is that teams are stuck—stuck in a state of disconnection. Everyone sees it and feels it. No one knows what to do about it.

Why Disconnection Matters

Consider the story of the cleaning crews for Japan's Shinkansen, the fast trains that speed at nearly 200 miles per hour (320 kph) just three minutes apart. At the Tokyo Station, a 22-person crew has to turn around a thousand-seat train, including wiping down tray tables, replacing seat covers, cleaning bathrooms, and collecting anything left behind. They manage to do all of this and more in just seven minutes.

It wasn't always like this, though. Previously the job was considered dirty, manual labor. Morale was low, and performance was poor, leading to frequent train delays.

Then, Tessei, the company managing the cleaning crews, introduced a program called "Shinkansen Theater." Dull uniforms were replaced with bright-red suits. Cleaners were allowed to speak with passengers. Recognition of colleague accomplishments was encouraged. And when work on a train is complete, the team now lines up to bow in unison to applause from the passengers about to board.

Many people like to point to the efficiency of Japanese work culture or the execution of well-coordinated work. But that misses the point. It wasn't until Tessei created a feeling of human connection that the pace of servicing trains picked up and delays plummeted. The cleaning crews were more connected to each other and to their mission. Even passengers felt more connected to the system and have started cleaning up after themselves more. Connection drove the engagement that led ultimately to efficiency, not the other way around.

Disconnection Puts Organizations at Risk

More madness than method, most meetings end with a lot of time wasted and little to show for the effort. People disengage as a result—from their teams, their jobs, and their organizations. For instance, according to a Capgemini[1] report, 56% of people feel disconnected from their colleagues because of remote work (that's a global average).

Having a strong connection to the mission of the group is an important factor in providing team cohesiveness, but it's not enough. Disconnection also happens through a series of small moments as people interact with each other. All of the eye rolls, "I told you so's," and other micromoments take a toll and add up. Little by little, our willingness to collaborate goes down, and teams get disconnected.

The consequences are real: People feel unseen, ideas are lost, and everyone gets frustrated. Or worse, alignment and engagement suffer, and teams lack clarity of direction. The entire reason teams form —that is, so that people become something greater together and do something they could never do apart—fails before it even gets started. Disconnection means the team can't do their best work.

Executives see the threat. They continue to hope the office, the traditional all-in-one solution for collaboration, holds the key. Surely bringing teams together in person will bring connection and collaboration back

Share of employees who felt disconnected from the organization and colleagues due to remote working worldwide in 2020, by country

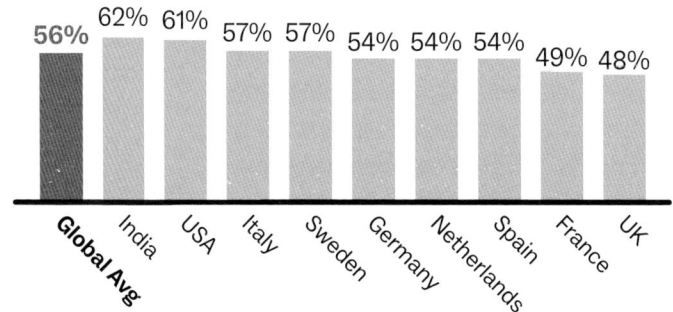

too. But going back is not going forward: The office is an obsolete fix to the collaboration problem. It's not enough to bring your brightest people together and wing it. And while tools and technology may keep us in touch, they are not enough to keep us connected.

Without connection, teams can't exist. Without teams, innovation is impossible. If leaders can't solve the disconnection problem, their teams can't do their best work. They can't innovate. Disconnection puts organizations at risk.

---

1   Capgemini. *The Future of Work: From Remote to Hybrid* (December 2020).

What Do We Mean by Connection?

Teams are made up of people, and the relationships between them directly influence the nature and quality of collaboration. This is not to say colleagues need to be friends or considered like "family." We have different types of relationships at work, but these person-to-person relationships are of critical importance for effective collaboration. Work is social, and incorporating personal connection is foundational for teams to function well.

But it goes deeper than that. More and more people want their work to be connected to a deeper purpose. These days people are willing to prioritize connection to the organization's purpose over an increased salary. At the same time, purpose-driven organizations are seeing greater attraction and retention of employees.

We can also refer to "connection" in relation to society and connection to nature and the planet

that people feel. These aspects of connection, too, are important to the conversation here.

Finally, there is a connection of work to life. We've long separated the two, trying to find work-life balance. This assumes they aren't connected when they are. What we do for a living is part of who we are. The Great Resignation of 2021 was also in part due to a resurgence of people connecting with their own lives. From this perspective, the future of work is really about the future of lifestyle.

Truth is, connection motivates us. Really. Don't believe us? Take author Jamil Zaki's, word for it. A professor of psychology at Stanford University, he shows that acts of kindness toward others help form stronger connections between people, which in turn inspires them to do more for themselves and for the world.[2] Connection isn't just about helping people feel

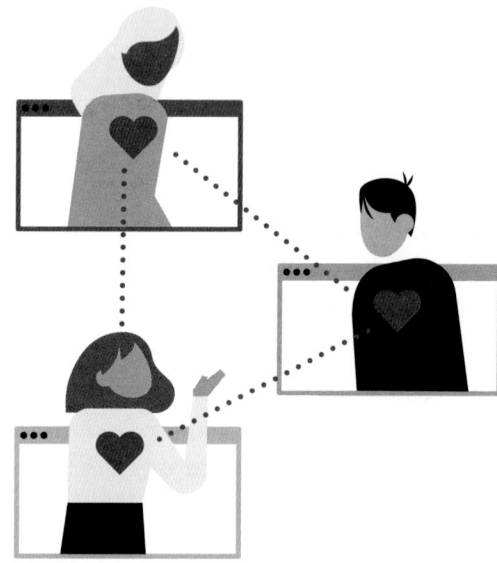

comfortable with colleagues, it's actually what moves them to do their best work.

Connection looks like believing in each other and believing in the work we do together. And if innovation comes from atypical alliances, then the ability to connect different people, different ideas, and different perspectives is critical to making it happen.

---

2   Jamil Zaki, *The War for Kindness: Building Empathy in a Fractured World* (2019).

Collaboration Now

To be sure, the study of workplace collaboration is not new. Research goes back decades, and consultants have been working to improve collaboration for a long time. A vast range of collaboration software and tools are available. What's missing is tying collaboration together at different levels—teams, tools, techniques, leadership, and more.

Disengaged workers who show up just to collect a paycheck will never reach their full potential and will ultimately reduce the overall innovation performance of the organization. Teams are drowning in real-time virtual interaction technology, from teleconferencing to instant messaging and everything in between, and it seems that as the ease of interacting with each other increases, productive, value-creating collaboration decreases.

In a 2009 interview with *Harvard Business Review* titled "Why Teams Don't Work," collaboration research pioneer J. Richard Hackman said: "Research consistently shows that teams underperform, despite all the extra resources they have. That's because problems with coordination and motivation typically chip away at the benefits of collaboration."

Collaborative intelligence, the approach described in this book, promises to change teams and collaboration for the better. It directly targets disconnection and seeks to build a healthy culture of collaboration.

Now is the time to make collaboration work for you.

Make Collaboration a Competitive Advantage

The good news is that there are clear signs that collaborative intelligence already works. Hundreds of teams *at companies like IBM, Autodesk, SAP, Booz Allen, and many others,* are already benefiting from the underlying principles in this book. We've been fortunate to have had the opportunity to witness the many benefits of better collaboration, including:

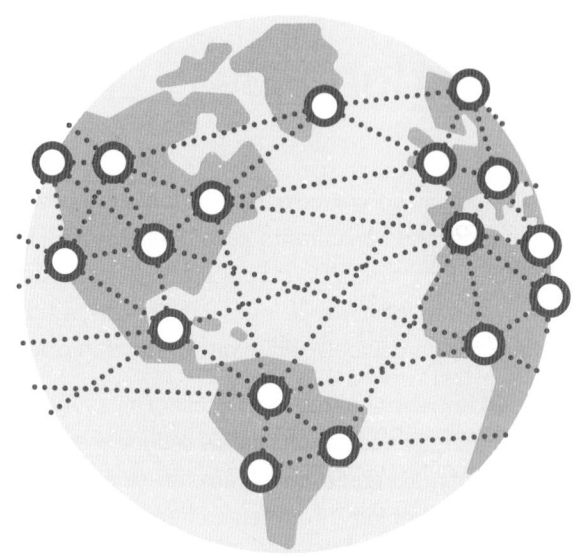

Enhanced group productivity. Teams can achieve more, faster when the all-too-common pitfalls of collaboration are minimized. It's not enough to just get individuals more productive; the productivity of the team is more critical in delivering results that matter.

Improved employee experience. The Great Resignation is a sign that the well-being of people in the workforce is suffering. The craft of collaboration design guides teams in building connections with each other and to the broader organization for a more inclusive work experience and fulfilling work.

Increased customer satisfaction. Because we're collaborating better, teams can come up with better solutions and serve customers better. Frontline staff—including consultants, customer success, and sales—need the know-how to enhance relationships in every engagement and customer experience. Once people collaborate better, everyone benefits, including customers.

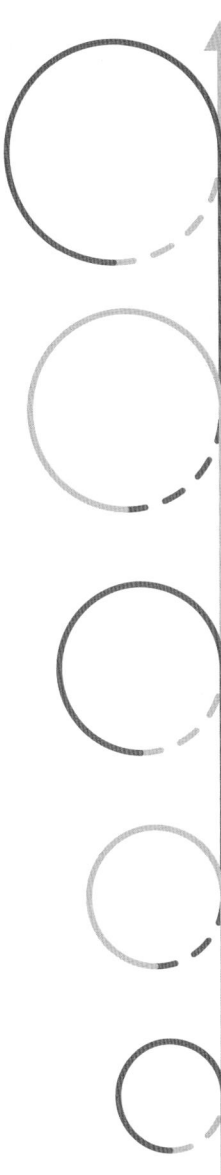

While improving collaboration benefits teams across the board, it's also delivers real business results. Time to market decreases and innovation quality is raised when teams collaborate more effectively.

Finally, dramatically improved collaboration doesn't just help businesses; it enables people in general to communicate and work together better. We believe core skills around Relational intelligence and using guided methods for problem-solving are catalysts for building connections between people, connections lead to greater innovation and a better society.

Approach Collaboration Holistically

We stand on the shoulders of giants. We acknowledge that many people are focused on better collaboration and want to recognize and thank all the researchers and practitioners who have created new paths in this field. Our take in this book is a way of thinking about collaboration that's centered around solving for disconnection and turning theory into practice.

What is clear from our research and experience with customers over the past decade is that to solve this problem, teams and companies need to take a comprehensive approach. This book describes the main building blocks of collaborative intelligence. Although there is a wealth of practical information included here, it's really the combination of factors that we'd like you to consider for your own journey.

In Chapter 1, we offer the principles we believe to be at the heart of collaboration that the rest of the system flows around. Chapter 2 explores the ability to build and navigate the productive interpersonal dynamics that exist any time a group of people come together—the foundation of productive collaboration.

With that groundwork laid, Chapter 3 introduces a new discipline that seeks to make collaboration more deliberate within and across teams: collaboration design. Guided methods (Chapter 4) are all of the exercises, methods, and techniques that get teams from point A to B in a directed manner. Collaboration based on guided methods makes teamwork both effective and fun. Chapter 5 switches gears to discuss collaboration spaces. It turns out that the quality and nature of the environment directly affect the quality and nature of collaboration and the outcomes. Paying close attention to the conditions and spaces in which collaboration happens.

Today, any one team—or any one worker for that matter—will move in and out of different temporal modes of working, from asynchronous work remotely to in-person work synchronously and hybrid variations in between. Chapter 6 lays out a framework for understanding the future of work from a more fluid perspective.

We believe collaboration can and should be measured so it can be improved. A 360-degree view of collaboration can directly be leveraged to not only measure the health of teamwork, but also guide teams toward healthier collaboration in the future. Chapter 7 introduces the idea of collaboration insights, or the range of metrics and data we can gain from team interactions.

Organizations must act now to set up a collaboration strategy, with a commitment to change from the top down. Chapter 8 will help leaders learn how to get teams collaborating more intelligently at scale and over time.

With collaborative intelligence, our aim is clear: We want nothing less than to start a movement toward more effective collaboration and healthier teams in organizations of all types and sizes around the world. We believe now is the time for teams to focus on how they collaborate for a more successful and rewarding work experience.

If changing the way we work together feels right to you—obvious even—we welcome you to join us in the movement.

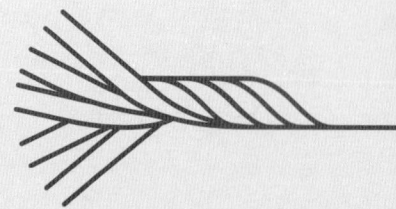

Recommended Reading

Collaborative Intelligence Community Space

Throughout the book you'll see references and highlights of some of our favorite works on the topics. Each chapter ends with a few of our top recommendations. You can also learn more at our hub of information and community activity, found here:

Find more online at
www.collaborativeintelligence.com

Chapter 1

Collaboration in Principle

Connecting the Genius of Your Teams

I f you're lucky, you've experienced what it feels like to be on a team. Clear on the mission and confident in each other's abilities, you lock arms with your fellow teammates and feel like you could conquer the world. Spirits are high, even when the challenges mount. Failures become moments that teach the team a new lesson. Members support each other when someone needs to take a break, and everyone celebrates together when milestones are reached.

Too often, that kind of peak experience at work is rare. It's more likely you feel lost in an organization, unclear on the "big picture," and unable to make a dent in the prevailing culture—a culture of disconnection that surrounds you.

Beyond Meeting Hygiene

Consider Sharon, a product designer in a large enterprise. Recently, a new, high-profile project brought her together with other smart and talented individuals from all over the company. Even before they met for the first time, the team shared a sense of enthusiasm. A casual glance at the roster showed many familiar names, all with reputations for innovation and knock-out successes. This was going to be fun, maybe even an opportunity to do something extraordinary!

Leadership wasted no time in sharing their sense of urgency with the team, as well as making it crystal clear just how high their expectations were. While sobering, the news bolstered Sharon's confidence. Just look at this team. Each person had done such great work in the past—what could go wrong?

The first two meetings were cordial, even though it didn't seem that very much was accomplished. But less than five minutes into the third meeting, all politeness evaporated. Certain voices became louder, while others grew steely or silent. Some quibbled about procedures, while others talked over each other. As the meeting drew to an uncomfortable close, Sharon's heart sank. They were not one step closer to their goals.

Someone suggested shifting technologies. They tried Zoom, Slack, and everything in between. But it wasn't helping. In fact, it seemed like the more ways the team had to interact with each other, the less value-creating collaboration happened.

There were so many brilliant individuals here—why was their productivity as a team so low?

We have all experienced this frustration. Discussions become circular. Colleagues jockey for attention as ego takes over. People disengage. Ideas are lost. There is no alignment, only frustration. Deadlines draw closer with little or no progress to report.

Between meetings, we might try a desperate search for "how to have better meetings" and come prepared with ideas like "Have an agenda! Polish those presentations! Capture everyones' action items!" But it's not enough. Though basic meeting hygiene is important, it's no substitute for thoughtful planning, leadership, and culture. No matter how talented a group of individuals might be, it takes intention and know-how—right from the beginning—to forge a highly collaborative team.

Sharon saw that the odds were low that this team was going to blow doors off any project. So she got to work putting together an approach that was thoughtful, intentional, and designed to remove luck from the collaboration equation.

She thought through a sequence of activities designed to build trust and bring out the full potential of everyone in the group. This approach would take the limited time a meeting affords into account. She'd select proven ways to guide interactions of the team, drawing out participation, removing ego from the equation, and focusing attention on the work.

Leaning gently into the camaraderie this new pattern-breaking experience would introduce, Sharon would pivot the group into a series of designed experiences or methods built to pull observations and

insights from each person. Like running plays in a game, each tailored to overcome specific obstacles and move a team down the field, the methods Sharon chose were crafted to activate and amplify the capacity of the team.

The plan worked! A few discussions ran longer than expected and everyone agreed that some additional work was required, but instead of leaving the experience tired and uninspired, the team left full of energy, clarity, and focus. These talented individuals were starting to function like a team.

Sharon's inbox began to fill up with 👍 messages and even an email thanking her at length for "creating a space where everyone gets heard." A sense of relief washed over her. Reviewing the visual artifact of the groups efforts on her screen, the results were undeniable.

Focused discussions turned into a preliminary road map and shared priorities for the week ahead. The team co-created a visual that cemented its alignment and progress. Sharon's team went from two months of indecision and frustration to a plan of action that everyone agreed upon in under a week, a nearly tenfold increase in velocity.

Sharon's manager, Abby, noticed this success too. Abby wasn't surprised that her best employee had pulled out a win when faced with a tough situation. In fact, she'd come to count on it. What Abby didn't expect, though, was that she'd now have to fill her brilliant employee's shoes. Sharon was moving on to an organization where her skills would bring more value and fulfillment. In her exit interview, Sharon expressed that while she appreciated the success of her team, she was frustrated by the pervasive dysfunction she'd experienced across teams.

Collaborate Smarter

It's not enough to bring your brightest people together and wing it. And while tools and technology may keep us in touch, they are not enough to keep us connected. As research by Google[1] has shown, how a team collaborates is more critical to innovation and generating outcomes than who is on the team. Whether you're in product, design, engineering, IT, consulting, innovation—or leading a company in the C-suite—when your organization fails to collaborate effectively, your best people not only can't do their best work, but they leave in search of better experiences.

The cost to your organization is real. It's also worse than you think. Some estimates show that businesses lose as much as $542 billion to pointless meetings.[2] Others show as much as 85% of employee time is wasted on inefficient collaboration.[3] And these costs are only the beginning. Because what's hard to measure is the value of a high-performing culture of collaboration. Organizations with teams that know how to collaborate effectively ship faster, innovate more often, and have happier customers.

Though the state of collaboration may be dire, there is hope. Instead of relying on a wing and a prayer, collaboration can be deployed systematically throughout your organization. Having observed thousands of teams across dozens of industries at Mural, a provider of tools and methods that help teams do their best work together, we've formalized a way of working that drives business outcomes. We call it collaborative intelligence.

Collaborative intelligence is a holistic approach to the way people work together. It fosters connections across all of the individuals working together in your teams—as well as outside of them—and unlocks their collective genius. Productivity is streamlined, time to market decreases, and innovation quality is raised when teams collaborate more effectively. Dramatically improved collaboration doesn't just help organizations; it enables people to communicate and work together better.

And it opens up a well of imagination that can allow for real innovation to happen. It can change the world.

1   Charles Duhigg. "What Google Learned From Its Quest to Build the Perfect Team," *New York Times* (Feb 2016). https://www.nytimes.com/2016/02/28/magazine/what-google-learned-from-its-quest-to-build-the-perfect-team.html

2   Doodle. *State of Meetings 2019 Report (2019).*

3   Rob Cross et al. "Collaboration Overload Is Sinking Productivity," *Harvard Business Review* (Sep 2021).

Principles of Collaboration

1
People Are Greater
Together Than Apart

2
Teams Can't
Exist Without
Connection

3
Collaboration
Should Not Be
Left to Chance

4
Collaborative
Spaces Power
Connected
Teams

5
Measuring
Collaboration is
Possible
—and Essential

Principle 1: People Are Greater Together Than Apart

Collaboration is individuals working together to achieve what would have otherwise been hard, if not impossible, to accomplish working alone.

It's the highest order of working together on a scale that begins with simple communication:

Communication doesn't even require a shared goal or a commitment to working together. In fact, communication is often one-way, in the form of messages broadcast to others with no interaction or dialogue between the communicating parties.

Coordination happens when there's a common goal, but it can happen without interaction between groups.

Cooperation demands participants have not only a shared purpose, but also a commitment to each other's success. But groups can work in concert without understanding each other's point of view.

Collaboration is teamwork between those with the same strong purpose and a dedication to each other as people. When individuals connect to each other in this way, they accept and learn from each other's perspectives and the whole becomes greater than the sum of the parts.

Collaboration is a mindset: an open willingness to come together to solve problems and engage in co-creation. It goes beyond a transactional way of working to a generative way of building relationships, where the lines between individual people blur as ideas and information are shared, iterated upon, and improved by the team. Collaboration produces unique outcomes that couldn't be achieved by anyone working alone.

There is no Thomas Edison tucked away solving all the great problems (even Edison had a team of "muckers" working alongside him, brokering ideas and tinkering together). Whether it's in the lab, on the field, in a classroom, or in a Zoom, two (or more) heads are better than one. People are greater together than they are apart, and hard problems are best tackled by teams.

Duncan Watts, a Wharton professor of operations, information and decisions, tested this theory. He and his research team conducted an experiment where both individuals and teams were instructed to complete tasks.[4] The teams were ultimately quicker at getting the job done, even if they arrived at the same result as the individuals. "Interestingly, what we found is that where teams really shine is in terms of efficiency," Watts said. "They were much faster, they generated more solutions, they generated faster solutions, and they explored the space of possibilities more broadly."[5]

What makes teams so much more than the sum of their parts? Individuals are limited to their own experiences and thoughts. Teams are a synthesis of unique backgrounds, perspectives, and ideas. One idea triggers another idea. One person's perspective challenges another's and opens a discussion. When that collective genius is activated, anything is possible.

4   Abdullah Almaatouq et al. "Task complexity moderates group synergy," *Proceedings of the National Academy of Sciences* (Sep 2021).

5   Knowledge@Wharton. "Are Teams Better Than Individuals at Getting Work Done?" [Audio podcast episode] (Oct 2021).

Principle 2: Teams Can't Exist without Connection

A group of people isn't a "team" just because someone calls it that. Teams are something more.

When you're a part of a team, you feel it. That sense of camaraderie, mutual trust and accountability, and the strength of being a part of something greater—that's connection.

Teams crave connection — can't exist without it. Being free to fire off ideas, troubleshoot problems, express concerns, and activate opportunities.

We talk to be heard. We listen to understand.

Ironically, more collaboration tools only compound the symptoms of disconnection. So why is it that today, when teams have channels galore and more ways than ever to communicate, we find it so very hard? Connection takes more than technology.

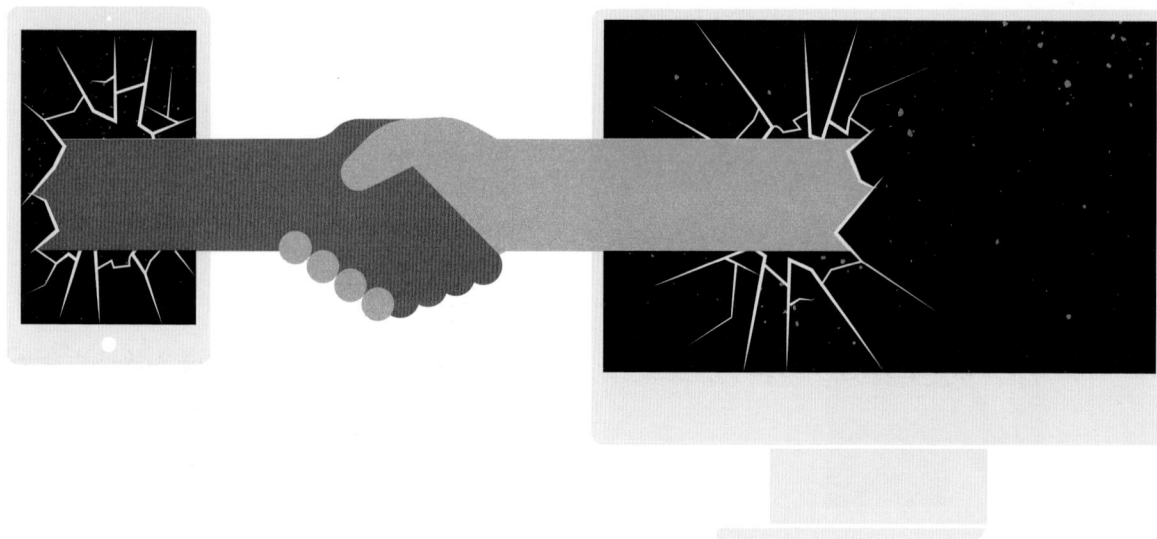

You have to take time and make space for connection—not just in yearly team-building activities but as an ongoing practice. Trust and care cannot exist in a vacuum. They're human emotions that only exist in relation to others.

A focus on the personal, relational—human—aspects of collaboration must become part of the basic operating system of teamwork. Relational intelligence is the ability to build and navigate the productive interpersonal dynamics that exist any time a group of people come together.

Principle 3: Collaboration Should Not Be Left to Chance

Product design isn't left to chance. Industrial design isn't left to chance. You don't leave critical work to chance.

So, when it comes to collaboration, why is the default strategy to throw people together and hope for the best?

So many leaders hope for "water cooler moments" and hallway collisions. They turn to creative approaches for designing office spaces in order to maximize the odds of spontaneous, serendipitous collaboration. During the pandemic, these traditional ways of encouraging serendipity became impossible. Physical offices were replaced with digital spaces. The focus on where work happened was replaced by figuring out *how* to make it happen. Organizations adopted the latest tools and technology to support collaboration. Still it wasn't enough.

Why? Because for teams to collaborate, they need reference points, common spaces, and common ways of working. Digital makes it possible to collaborate from anywhere, but it doesn't automatically result in these commonalities. And as work continues to shift to digital

territories, designing how—and not where—work happens is becoming the critical function.

Being intentional about collaboration and designing teamwork requires a new approach. It's a topic that's fundamental and wide-ranging, serious enough to deserve its own discipline: collaboration design.

Collaboration designers bring purpose and intention to the collaboration process, inspiring teams to connect and innovate. The discipline of collaboration design takes direct aim at the isolation and disengagement many people feel. The craft supports the psychological needs of teams with relational intelligence. Using playful, provocative methods of visual thinking, collaboration design helps teams take ideas from imagination to activation.

Collaboration design codifies proven ways of working from design thinking, Agile methodologies, and other pioneers in facilitation.

Rather than design office spaces, it's time to design collaborative experiences—and empower teams to do their best work together.

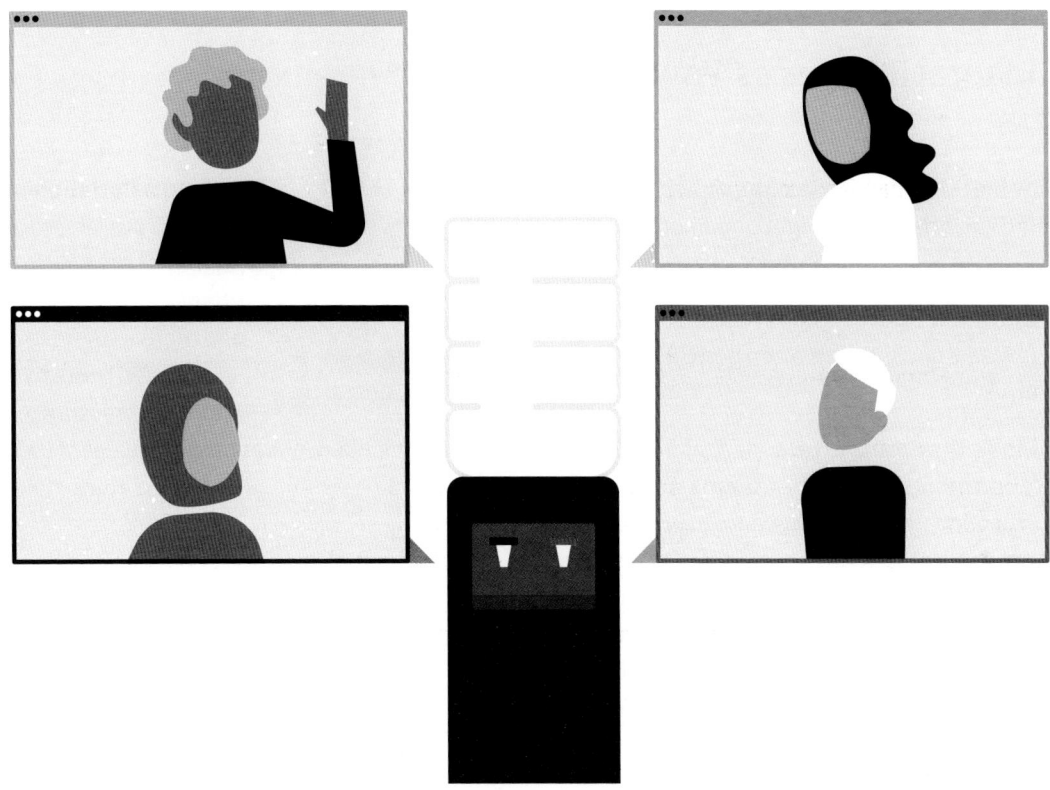

Principle 4: Collaborative Spaces Power Connected Teams

Decades of research show that you must enable the right conditions for successful collaboration. So what are the right conditions for true collaboration?

Common Space. A common space may be physical or digital. It's often both at the same time.

Most importantly, true, purpose-built collaboration spaces offer teams a place for exceptional teamwork because they are accessible and inclusive. These spaces amplify the strengths of team members—they don't average them out. When an environment excludes any member of a team, the team can't realize its full potential. Collaboration spaces reduce bias, promote risk-taking, make it easy to play with ideas, reward imagination, and support the courage to contribute.

Common spaces make it possible for a team to have shared reference points. Teams working in a common space can go from simply using communication channels to co-creating a shared reality.

Dynamic Communication. Despite countless channels available for communication, modern teams still struggle to communicate effectively. Phone, email, chat, video calls, documents, and more all impose uniquely stringent, often unintended limits to communication. Just as often, the pressure to use any particular form of communication—or, at other times, all of them—muddies messages.

People need to be free to communicate dynamically: to be able to share ideas and insights thoughtfully and meaningfully in whatever form is most appropriate to the content—and the person. "Dynamic communication" can take the form of individual words and concepts jotted out on sticky notes. It can also look like diagrams or visual metaphors. It can and often is both and more. What's crucial is that dynamic communication adapts to the needs of the team when it must convey never-before-expressed ideas, allowing information to be shared in a way that it can be questioned, adjusted, and ultimately, understood.

Time to Team. Collaboration takes time. Because collaboration necessarily means two or more people working together, time spent working together can be costly. It's also a finite, valuable resource that not every team member can access equally. Differences in modalities—synchronous, asynchronous, in-person, remote, hybrid—time zones, workloads, and other needs means that time spent working together must be managed with intention. It's too important to misuse.

More productive and inclusive collaborative experiences become possible when teams unbundle time into synchronous and asynchronous collaboration. But to make the best use of dynamic working time requires a particular set of skills.

"The great enemy of communication, we find, is the illusion of it."

– William Whyte

Principle 5: Measuring Collaboration Is Possible—and Essential

How much does your company invest in meetings today? Let's say you have 10,000 employees who spend 50% of their time in meetings. If the average salary is $100,000 per year, that's an annual investment of $500 million… in meetings. With so much at stake, measuring that investment is no longer a nice-to-have: it's a must-have.

And in order to shape the way our teams and organizations collaborate, we have to be able to measure it, observe and analyze trends, and learn from what's working. Because collaboration is happening more and more in digital spaces, data about collaboration effectiveness is prevalent. But it's underused. Collaboration insights turn raw data about how teams are working together into actionable intelligence, responsibly and with respect for privacy.

There are different levels of insights we can get from measuring collaboration:

Individual. Collaboration insights help individuals better understand and assess their own collaboration performance and evaluate concrete actions they can take to improve.

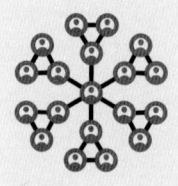

Organization. At the company level, see how teams connect and interact. For example, anonymized views of collaboration insights can provide input into the general effectiveness of collaboration and can even show which teams are most likely to come up with good ideas.

Team. For teams of 10 members or more, anonymized and aggregated collaboration insights help assess and improve collaboration within their group. For example, after a workshop or meeting, teams could learn how engaged people were or how well methods were employed.

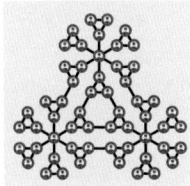

Ecosystem. Finally, collaboration insights also help spot global trends in collaboration design, providing insight into how changes in the way work is done impact collaboration as well as how to collaborate better externally.

Welcome to the Renaissance of Teamwork

We recognize that researchers and practitioners alike have been striving for better collaboration for decades and decades. And after combing through dozens of the key resources about collaboration from the past 40 years, we've also conducted our own primary research with dozens of workers and thought leaders in the field. From all of these inputs, patterns have emerged.

Collaboration doesn't have to look like an endless slog through meaningless meetings and pointless presentations. Real collaboration is not the result of chance. And collaboration is not an end point, it's a means to an end. Innovation, a job well done, a product launch, or whatever the desired outcome, you must be able to know enough about the way your business collaborates if you want to grow it.

This will require change. To achieve a more innovative organization, leaders must get smarter about how they help teams work. People will have to learn new ways of working. Executives will have to acquire new ways of understanding so they can effectively manage how teams collaborate. Everyone must start paying attention to what kind of collaboration leads to innovation.

The way we collaborate has changed. To keep up, teamwork needs to become more productive, faster, and smarter. Collaborative intelligence imagines a better future for work.

Recommended Reading

Amy Edmonson, *Teaming* (2014)

By focusing on the act of working together, Edmonson shows us that teams are verbs (teaming) instead of nouns (teams). This volume is packed with insights and backed by extensive research, while remaining rooted in practical examples and application of the principles of teamwork. Edmonson's work on psychological safety is particularly deep and relevant, often cited as a key source on the topic.

Richard Hackman, *Leading Teams* (2002)

This is a classic book on collaboration from one of the pioneers in the field. Don't let the publication date fool you: This is still relevant and fresh. His identification of core elements of collaboration have influenced future models, including ours.

Daniel Coyle, *The Culture Code* (2018)

This bestseller demystifies teams and team building in a fresh way, looking deep into the core human elements that drive culture. In particular, Coyle focuses on three skills his research has highlighted that teams need in order to get to the next level of collaboration: build safety, share vulnerability, and establish purpose. From Navy SEALs to IDEO to the San Antonio Spurs, the author provides real-world examples and evidence that are relatable and practical.

Dov Seidman, *How: Why How We Do Anything Means Everything* (2011)

Dov Seidman, a prominent author and thought leader in business, presents a compelling case for transformation on how work gets done and why that's the next big competitive advantage. It is no longer just what you do that sets you apart from the rest, but how you do it.

 Find more online at
www.collaborativeintelligence.com

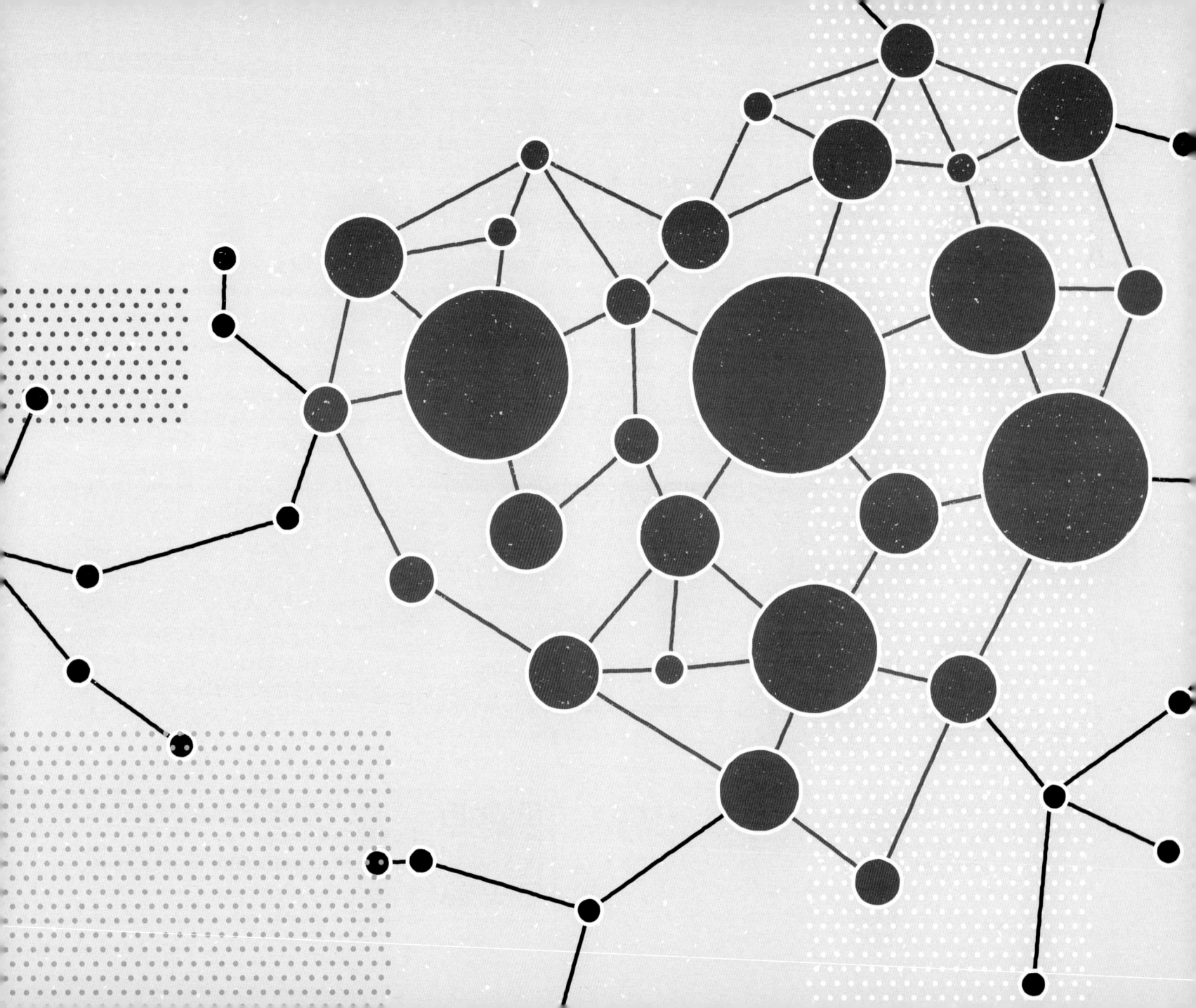

Chapter 2

Relational Intelligence

The Human Aspect of Collaboration

After working for the same entertainment company for 17 years, Fernanda was crying tears of joy for the first time.

The reason she was so happy? A huge in-person event celebrating a global brand relaunch had been canceled. The 17-year-veteran in Brazil had worked hard on the roll-out with her whole team. The entire global organization the team worked for had as well.

So why did the derailment of this massive effort lead to her feeling like she belonged and was connected to a team more than ever?

In the past, they'd done these types of large-scale roll-outs in person. At enormous expense, they'd fly many people in from around the world with the idea that they'd be more productive and connect better when face to face. It seemed like a logical assumption, but it left out a large cohort of people. Those who didn't get flown in still attended, but only over a conference call and from a range of different time zones. Because of the size of the company, privileging in-person meetings meant excluding some team members.

For over a decade, Fernanda had seen this first-hand: time differences meant that it was often late at night in Singapore when she and her team joined these calls, and her typically vocal team tended to become mere observers of the "interactions."

Then the COVID-19 pandemic changed how teams worked together.

Because of travel and gathering restrictions, for the first time, the brand relaunch wasn't held in-person. Instead it was held completely remotely and asynchronously. Really, the organization felt lucky it was able to put an event together at all during those challenging times.

Something unexpected happened during their collaboration: Participation from locations that had been distant from previous events increased dramatically. A wider variety of people in different types of teams and places felt more connected, both with each other and with the problems they were trying to solve. Even better, the group of people was more diverse in terms of perspective, background, and geographic location. As a result of the increased number of voices included, ideas and concepts were more robust. The content was more globally relevant. And by better connecting teams—even distributed around the world—the speed and quality of their output increased.

Fernanda found that she was able to better leverage her expertise during the event. And as a result, her team became more and more engaged with the global effort and ultimately performed better. The improvement wasn't just due to better videoconferencing technology. The fact that all of the teams were collaborating in the same way—none more distant than others—gave Fernanda, at last, a sense of belonging.

"For the first time in my career, I felt I had a seat at the table," she said.

This wasn't just luck. The team leads stepped up to design an intentional collaboration experience that created the conditions for Fernanda's voice to be included, regardless of her location. It turns out that there is an upward spiral of positive effects when teams get connected and feel included. Being distributed and connected with digital technology is an incredible opportunity. But it's only a benefit if you take the time to connect in a deliberate way and pay attention to relationships between team members.

Trust Falls Won't Solve Your Problems

You don't hire machines. You hire people. And people are complicated Any attempt at collaboration must explicitly recognize and pay attention to the human aspects of teamwork. Do otherwise—treat people like machines or relegate relationship-building to a once-a-year offsite team-building exercise—and the inevitable result is disconnected, unproductive, unhappy teams.

We call this focus on connection between people "relational intelligence". Getting it right makes our teams function better. And smarter.

Relational intelligence involves the ability to be aware of and understand your own and others' values, needs, styles, and interests.

In essence, relational intelligence deals with the interpersonal, human aspects of team collaboration.

Work relationships are social in their own right, and these social aspects matter. They drive effective teamwork, innovation, and the overall mental well-being of an organization.

Working together on a team isn't easy—especially in today's remote and hybrid world. Despite countless ways to communicate, teams still struggle to collaborate, much less innovate.

Our own research shows that the biggest concern of people working in remote teams is a lack of social connection with colleagues. In the midst of the pandemic in 2020, people indicated in our yearly survey that they missed social interactions with colleagues most.

Other research confirms that social aspects are critical to modern teams. The authors of an article in the MIT Sloan Management Review found that with hybrid workforces now common, deliberate attention must be paid to social connection in remote and hybrid

What frustrates you most when collaborating remotely?

Social Interaction	
Spontaneity	
Communication	
Creativity	
Time Zones	
Technology	
Options for Tools	
Culture	
Re-finding	
Process	
Other	

Results for Mural's survey on remote collaboration for 2020. 403 total respondents.

work: "Remote work is now so widespread that organizational leaders must be prepared to manage the negative impact on social climate that can result. This will require conscientious attention to ensuring support from managers and colleagues in both the office and at home."[1]

In order to solve for disconnection in organizations, human relationships and social aspects of work must be brought into play. Practically speaking, relational intelligence entails getting present to one another, listening, and reflecting. It's also about learning how to share creative ideas and connecting with team members on a meaningful level. And it's not a one-time thing. You must make it a regular part of how you collaborate.

That starts with deepening your own relational awareness as a collaborator.

1   Caroline Knight, Doina Olaru, Julie Anne Lee, and Sharon K. Parker. "The Loneliness of the Hybrid Worker," *MIT Sloan Management Review* (May 2022) https://sloanreview.mit.edu/article/the-loneliness-of-the-hybrid-worker.

The Collaboration Mindset

Simply put, collaboration requires us to work with others. This cannot happen until we recognize our own strengths, weaknesses, and styles of working.

Collaboration starts with the right mindset and extends outward. Three factors most influence our relationships within a group:

Curiosity. Every collaboration is an opportunity to learn. Team members need curiosity—not only about the topic and challenge at hand— but about each other, and they should check egos and biases at the door. The best collaborators are perpetual beginners, always coming to their teams with an open mind, a readiness to accept new ideas and find solutions together.

Respect. Every member of a team must afford the others the emotional and physical space to express their thoughts and ideas, seeking understanding, even when what's shared may seem unusual or even unpopular. The alternative is disastrous, not only because of the negative climate created but the loss of the very ideas and opportunities for creative collisions that power collaboration. Respect is distinct from trust, which implies a sense of earned reliability and truth. While trust is a consistent aspect of high-performing teams, it's not necessarily a prerequisite for collaboration. Otherwise, we'd never be able to work with individuals we've never met before.

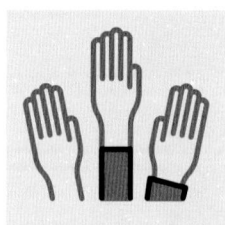

Willingness. True collaboration happens at a deeper level of connection. If team members don't intend to work together, meaningful collaboration won't happen. Sure, a group of people can be brought together to discuss the topics at hand, and they may even cooperate and coordinate with each other. But if there isn't a genuine intent within each team member to work with others, we're really just performing "collaboration theater."

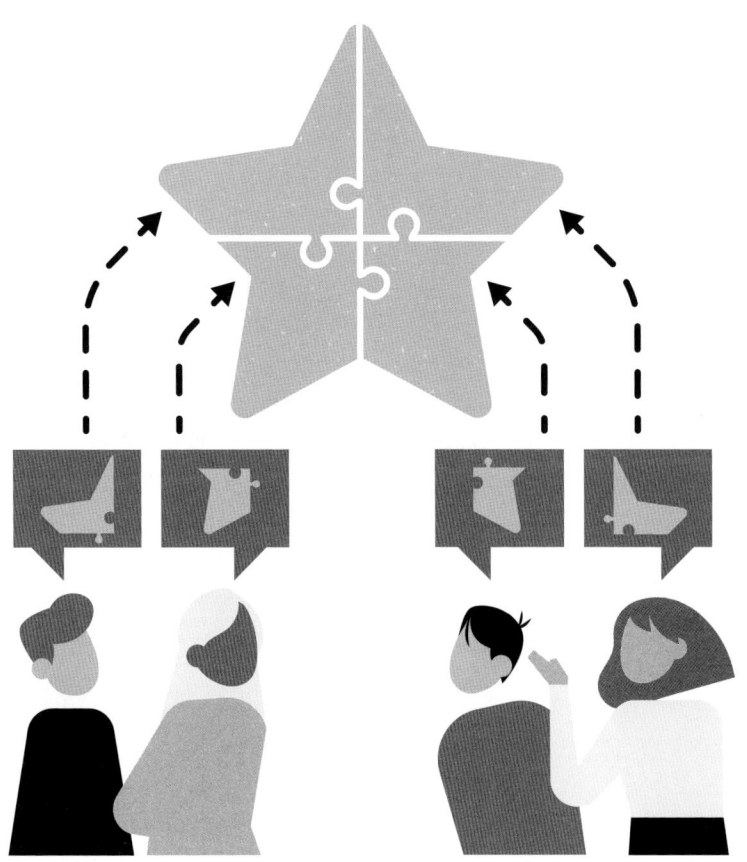

Intrinsic Motivation

Together, these three factors determine a team member's readiness for collaboration. Patrick Lencioni sums it up well in his book *The Five Dysfunctions of a Team* (2002): "Great teams ensure that everyone's ideas are genuinely considered, which then creates a willingness to rally around whatever decision is ultimately made by the group."

These qualities add up to something more than the sum of their parts, too: an intrinsic motivation for collaboration, a passion within you or something you believe in. This differs from extrinsic motivation, which is doing something to win an award or avoid a punishment, or the desire to achieve something based on external pressure. If you consistently cultivate your own curiosity, respect, and willingness for meeting others where they are, being a productive member of a team is its own reward.

Meeting of the Minds

It might be obvious, but from a collaboration standpoint, it's also wonderful: People don't all think alike.

If collaboration is ultimately an alliance of many minds, diversity adds to its effectiveness. In fact, we've noticed a pattern: When teams are "stuck" it's usually due to a lack of diverse perspectives. Bring in an outside opinion or point of view, and things tend to get unstuck. Real innovation happens when a heterogenous alliance of minds forms.

To support—or be part of—teams working together, it's critical to have a basic sense of the ways in which people think can fundamentally differ.

Team Needs

Once you've begun to understand your own thinking styles and the ways others tend to work, it's possible to approach the relationships between team members.

Abraham Maslow's famous hierarchy of needs focuses on the individual in society. But in a culture of collaboration, the unit of analysis is the team itself. So our model of team needs both extends and inverts Maslow's. Team actualization is the ultimate goal, and to get there first requires forming a sense of team safety and team belonging.

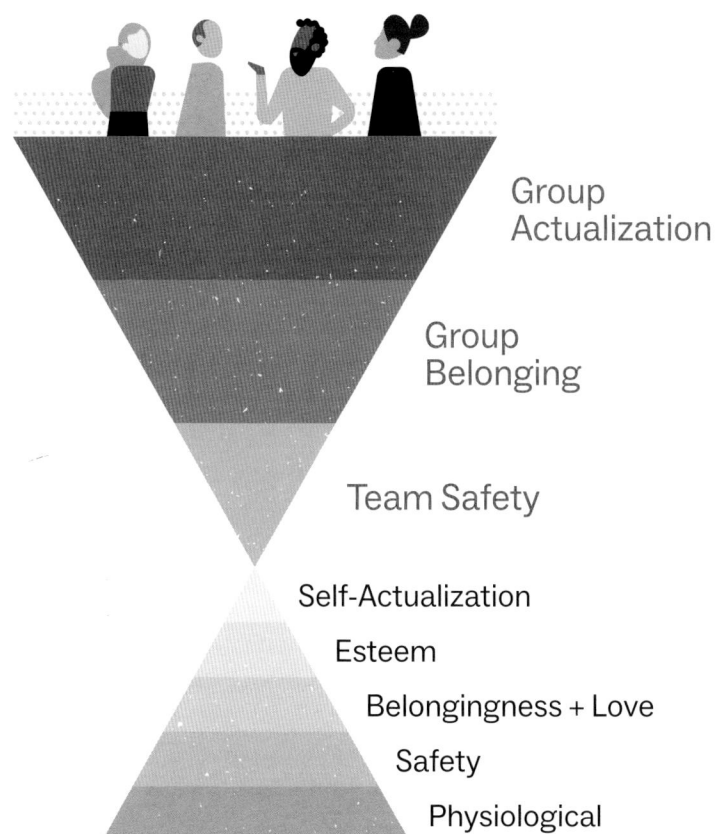

Group
Actualization

Group
Belonging

Team Safety

Self-Actualization

Esteem

Belongingness + Love

Safety

Physiological

Team Safety

Psychological safety describes an overall team climate staked on mutual respect in which people are comfortable speaking their minds, taking risks, and trying out new things without fear of repercussions. High-performing teams have a great deal of psychological safety built into their standard mode of operation.

Psychological safety isn't just about consensus and harmony within the team. On the contrary, it's psychological safety that enables team members to challenge each other. Teams have to be able to disagree for imagination to flourish. It's possible to be provocative and empathetic at the same time.

The phrase "psychological safety" was popularized by Harvard Business School professor Amy C. Edmondson in her book *Teaming* (2012). Her definition of psychological safety is straightforward: "A shared belief that the team is safe for interpersonal risk-taking." When there is no psychological safety, people check out, and imagination shuts down.

Psychological safety isn't absolute nor is it something leaders can simply "set and forget." A lack of safety will exist in any team at any time to different degrees because psychological safety is situational, varying from interaction to interaction among team members. Concerns about psychological safety are an ongoing aspect of teams collaborating.

So the real question is how its presence affects contributions from the team. Collaborative intelligence strives to address psychological safety in crafting team experiences and creating an environment that fosters participation, session by session, interaction by interaction.

Generating psychological safety for your teams doesn't have to be a mystery. Alla Weinberg, author of *A Culture of Safety* (2020), recommends taking some simple steps to get started:

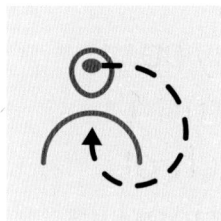

Shift from YOU to I. Demonstrate good collaboration behaviors by avoiding the blame game. Instead, frame your discussion from the "I" perspective. Keep your point of view and language focused on your own experience, and encourage others to do so as well.

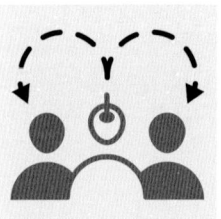

Get vulnerable. Don't be afraid to share what's happening for you in the moment and how collaborating together affects you, both practically and emotionally. Show others on your team that it's OK to talk about the experiences together, even if they feel exposed and vulnerable in doing so.

Reflect. Invite others on the team to share what's going on for them in the moment, as well as what past experiences have shaped their behavior and decision-making. Take time to think about how things are going and what you can do as a group to make it better.

"When a team has trust, they operate together as a cohesive unit. They look for ways to help each other, and they have healthy relationships with each other.... A remote team that doesn't trust each other is doomed."

– Lisette Sutherland, Director of Collaboration Superpowers

Just consider how teams at Atlassian build trust and psychological safety. For a lot of people, the sudden shift to remote work in early 2020 was a shock to the system. The boundary between work and home was not just blurred, but decimated, and it was harder for team members to feel connected. Eugene Chung, R&D team coach at Atlassian, set about designing a workshop to solve this problem. The result was the Work Life Impact Play, a method you can use to build psychological safety and identify the right support for your team.

Eugene told us that "focusing on skills of true empathy, of being able to understand each other, being able to adapt with each other, and really get you to this point having this deeper sense of trust and connection with your teams, this resilience on teams ... [these] are the skills we're trying to build up now."

One key way to build a sense of belonging is to acknowledge individual contributions. Take time to recognize achievements. The strongest teams we've observed also celebrate wins together. This need not be elaborate award ceremonies with prizes or bonuses. Just a simple "good job" or "thanks for your help" now and then goes a long way toward belonging.

Group Belonging

Sure, skill and talent matter: Each person needs to bring their best self to the table. But talent alone doesn't make a high-performing team.

In sports, we see time and time again: A roster of top athletes that everyone assumes will dominate the competition ends up losing to teams without superstars who play better together.

A virtuoso musician has to be proficient at their own instrument. But playing in a band requires a different type of facility—listening, adjusting, and reacting in real time—abilities that go beyond individual technical ability.

The *"War on Talent"* that broke out in the 1990s proved to be counterproductive. Stanford's Jeffrey Pfeffer, for one, has shown in study after study that a fixation on talent only undermines existing teams inside an organization, often leading to a corrosive culture.[2]

Malcolm Gladwell showed how that kind of competitive dynamic contributed to Enron's downfall.[3]

Having the right talent is a good thing. But the truth is that talent will be ineffective within dysfunctional teams. Fostering a culture of collaboration requires a sense of belonging: The people on your team need to not just be affiliated with one another, but to also know that they share commonalities. Belonging requires that a bond be somehow made manifest. In collaboration, that often takes the form of alignment.

Alignment is a key factor in creating cohesive teams. Simply agreeing on your purpose isn't enough. In fact, being aligned doesn't always mean being in complete agreement. Teams and companies need to coordinate on how they will act to fulfill their purpose. Not just on a tactical, day-to-day level but on a strategic level.

Ryan McKeever, writer and CX leader, puts it like this: "Alignment means everyone can support a decision as if it were their own, even if they might have done something different if they ruled the world....[4] Agreement, on the other hand, requires a higher degree of commitment from each person on the team. Agreement means there is unanimity of opinion."

---

2   Jeffrey Pfeffer, "Fighting the War for Talent is Hazardous to Your Organization's Health," Stanford Business working paper (2001).

3   Malcolm Gladwell, "The Talent Myth," New Yorker (2002).

4   Ryan McKeever, "How Aligned Is Your Organization?" *Huffington Post* (2013).

Group Actualization

Mission statements like *"to be the best in our industry"* or *"to reach half a billion dollars in revenue"* are hollow and self-serving. And they aren't motivating.

Once purpose goes beyond the organization, engagement and motivation increase. That might explain why we're seeing a shift in how organizations approach purpose, expanding the concept beyond just profit and business success. For instance, the concept of "shared value" as developed by Michael E. Porter anchors purpose as a competitive advantage. It's a win-win approach: You'll not only engage employees and customers in a new way, you'll also outperform your competitors.

In order for work to be meaningful, wrote Malcolm Gladwell,[5] it needs to have three characteristics:

Autonomy. No one wants to be micromanaged—another reason trust is so important in the workplace.

Complexity. It's hard to stay engaged at work when we're not being challenged. In fact, boredom is the number one reason people consider leaving their jobs, a survey by Korn Ferry suggests.[6]

Connection between effort and reward. It's gratifying to see the impact of our work. It's even more satisfying to be rewarded for it. This one's all about extrinsic motivation: getting fairly compensated for the work we do.

Whether at the company or team level, when purpose is meaningful, alignment is easier too. Aligning each team with an overarching purpose and then giving it the autonomy to act gives rise to group actualization, the ultimate state of team fulfillment.

---

5   Malcolm Gladwell, Outliers (2011).

6   Korn Ferry, "Breaking Boredom: Job Seekers Jumping Ship for New Challengers in 2018, According to Korn Ferry Survey," press release, January 4, 2018, https://www.kornferry.com/about-us/press/breaking-boredom-job-seekers-jumping-ship-for-new-challenges-in-2018-according-to-korn-ferry-survey.

Relationship Goals

Unleashing Your Collective Imagination

There's another way to characterize the ultimate in group actualization: collective imagination. But the kind of imagination we're talking about here isn't about fairy tales and magic dragons; it's about finding ways to solve the world's toughest problems.

Does everyone understand their team's purpose, and their own? Can they see the impact their work is having? If they can—if purposeful alignment is coupled with the kind of psychological safety that encourages risk-taking—then imagination can flourish in an organization.

But the converse is true, too: regardless of how well the team gets along, and no matter how much they trust each other, it's nearly impossible to activate a collective imagination if your purpose is murky.

Business growth isn't just about number crunching to maximize profit: Increasingly, companies that prosper will distinguish themselves from competitors by first out-imagining them. Sure, experimentation and delivery are part of the equation, but true differentiation begins with imagination. It's core to innovation. Growth starts with imagination.

Artificial intelligence (AI) and other technologies won't get you there: They might take the "thinking" off your shoulders, but not the ability to imagine a better future. Now more than ever, businesses need to tap into the power of team imagination.

Imagination doesn't only fuel growth, it also drives a team's ability to change themselves. Imagination is key in finding new ways of working together. With imagination, teamwork becomes engaging, productive, and fun.

> With imagination, "Can you see what I mean?" goes from a prayer to a process.

We believe that innovation and change can happen anywhere, as long as great minds can be connected, collaborating toward a common goal. No longer are only decision-makers responsible for innovation: Everyone can contribute. It starts with relationships—each other—and leads to imagination, an endless resource that your team can tap into right now.

This is why we implore you to move to make collaboration more deliberate. Because you can do so in a way that harnesses the potential of

Recommended Reading

Alla Weinberg, *A Culture of Safety* (2020)

This thin volume packs a powerful punch of to-the-point arguments for growing a culture of psychological safety along with practical ways to get there. "Without safety, we literally can't think, collaborate or innovate," writes Weinberg. This no-nonsense exploration of the topic is a must-have for anyone interested in improving psychological safety on their teams.

Anne Rød and Marita Fridjhon, *Creating Intelligent Teams* (2020)

Based on Relationship Systems Intelligence, the study of how group members are networked and connected together, this book is both inspirational and practical.

Michael Lee Stallard et al., *Connection Culture* (2020)

Stallard and colleagues take an in-depth look at the importance of creating a culture of connection in any organization. The basis for their working model of a connected culture relies on three dimensions: vision, values, and voice. This book is not only inspirational, it's also well researched and very practical.

Stephen MR Covey, *The Speed of Trust* (2018)

Trust makes the world go around—literally, according to Covey—and its critical to team collaboration. Building trust starts with relational intelligence and creating the conditions in which trust can flourish. This volume takes an extremely deep dive into the topic trust, including research, examples, advice, assessments, and more across nearly 350 pages.

collective imagination as teams come together to solve problems and innovate. Imagination is one of the incredible functions of the human brain: the ability to see things differently, to conceive of a future that doesn't yet exist. Homo sapiens are the only species able to think counterfactually, and from this perspective, human imagination underlies progress in the world.

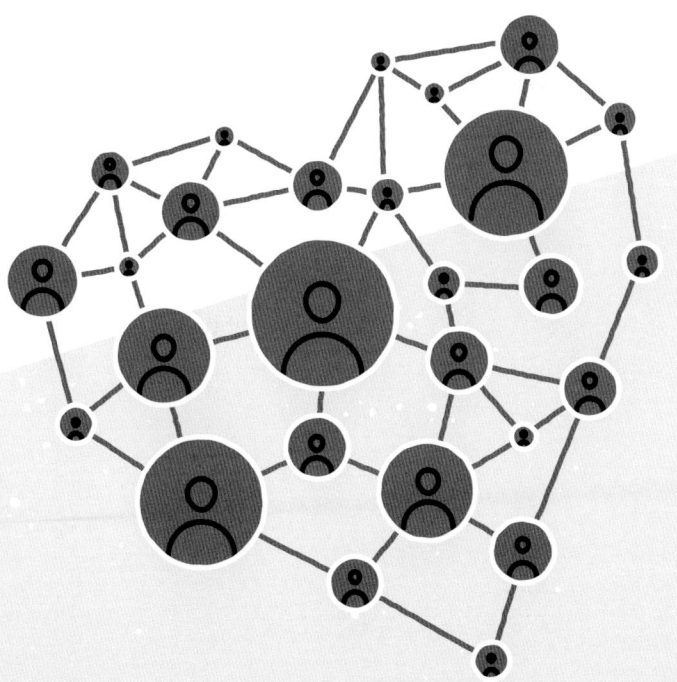

Find more online at
www.collaborativeintelligence.com

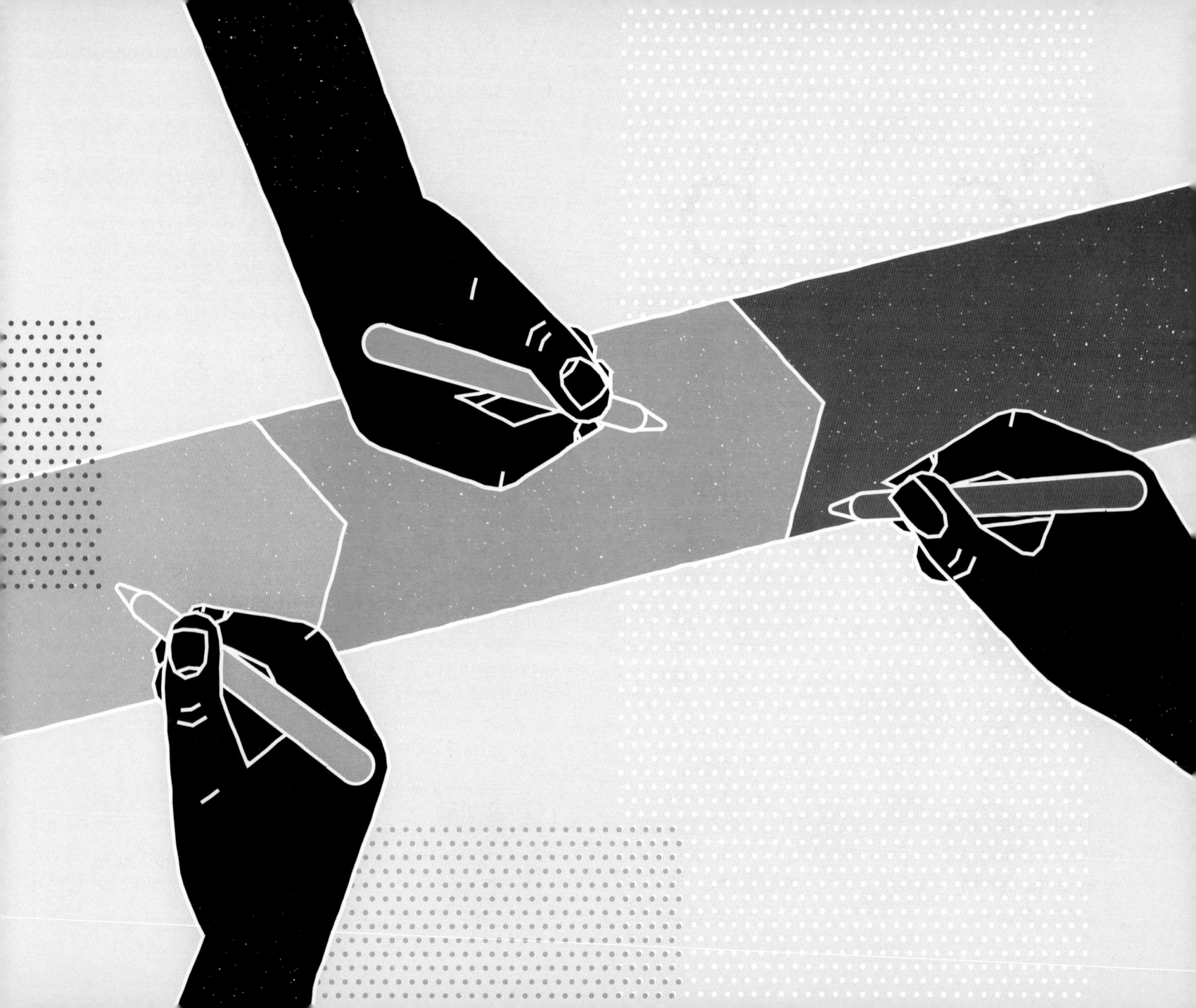

Collaboration
Design

Making The Collaboration Experience Deliberate

"Have an agenda."

That's the secret to holding better meetings, right?

But think about the last meeting you were in with an agenda. Did it go well? We mean really well—no egos and no politics getting in the way of achieving the team's goals. It probably didn't.

Having an agenda is good table stakes, but it won't fix a badly organized, poorly run meeting.

There's much more to consider. Are the right people invited? Are they able to participate meaningfully, to contribute? How will you lead so that people feel engaged—connected and wanting to be part of the work being done? How will everyone know

progress was made? And how well will the collaboration of the team work over time?

The list goes on, but these kinds of issues have to be worked out again and again when leaders leave collaboration to chance. There's no thoughtfulness, no consideration, no design to how the collaboration should unfold.

Who Can Fix Bad Meetings?
(Hint: Anyone)

Someone has to raise their hand to guide the team. It doesn't have to be a lot of work. Sometimes a simple nudge is all it takes: Just leading a warm-up, ensuring fair turn-taking, and providing solid follow-up can change the dynamics of an entire team and drive better results. It's about paying attention to collaboration as the collaboration happens, either in real time or when working apart. Because here's the thing: Collaboration happens whether it's deliberately guided or not.

As workplaces become less hierarchical and more reliant on team imagination, the ability to design productive collaboration is quickly becoming a skill everyone on any knowledge-work team needs to have. Equipping everyone in an organization with the ability to improve team interactions will simply lead to more innovation faster.

Collaboration designers don't have to be subject matter experts or professional facilitators. At its fundamental level, collaboration design is about helping people go forward. And anyone can do that. From this perspective, you may very well already be a collaboration designer and not know it.

What exactly is collaboration design? It's a new discipline that seeks to democratize methods and better ways of working into learnable skills that anyone can acquire. It's about working with the team, meeting them where they are, and helping them accomplish their goals.

Facilitation and collaboration design are particularly close cousins, but they differ in some very important ways.

Collaboration design can be formal or informal. Collaboration design is both a general skill set and a formalized role. We envision professionals specialized and certified in collaboration design, but anyone leading teams and conversations can learn and develop collaboration design skills— from individual contributors to managers and beyond.

Collaboration design will be an embedded function. Every team benefits from collaboration design know-how, which is why we see this new field materializing as a foundational skill that will be widespread across organizations in the future. As a result, champions will emerge to guide teams from their own ranks.

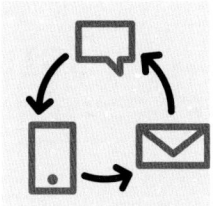

Collaboration design leverages asynchronous communication. Typically, facilitation happens in live meetings in real time, though it might occasionally include some preparatory or follow-up tasks. Collaboration design goes beyond these limitations to include asynchronous collaboration habits and behaviors of the team as well as synchronous meetings.

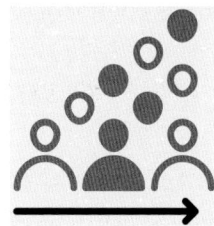

Collaboration design considers team development and evolution over a longer term. Solving for disconnection in teams doesn't happen overnight or even in a few sessions. Collaboration design is all about building the relationships between team members over time and considering the health of the team in the long run.

At its core, collaboration design requires attention and empathy. Pulling from Agile practices, design thinking, and facilitation as well as the fields of organizational design, psychology, and employee experience, collaboration designers stack the deck in favor of "aha moments" by catalyzing conversations, relationships, and intelligent collaboration.

What Does a Collaboration Designer Do?

Consider Blake: He came up through the ranks of client-facing teams at the global consultancy where he works. Blake ran a lot of workshops with clients and also worked closely with internal teams to plan accounts. But he noticed things were disjointed, particularly the client experience.

Like everybody else, Blake's work relied on meetings. And when the meetings didn't go well, work didn't go well. "People were trying to run meetings like they would offline, but online," he told us. "And scheduling a meeting happened way too easily here—people gathered at the drop of a hat whether it was needed or not."

Blake was already interested in topics around the future of work and facilitation in general, and he got certified in design thinking methods with LUMA. He also saw that as greater flexibility in work location became the norm, no team could assume everyone would be present in an office for a given meeting or workshop, and they'd have to be able to survive with a mix of participants at all times—some in-person and some remote. As he puts it, "Hybrid requires different etiquette within the group. There has to be an implicit awareness of each others' ability to participate, and getting the right habits is key."

It wasn't long before Blake was recognized as someone who could make teams work better together. Leaders found real value in the example he set. After the company re-orged into new pillars, they created new cross-functional roles, including dedicated collaboration designers. Now Blake and his small team improve collaboration frontstage as facilitators as well as doing backstage work with a type of "collaboration ops." They select common methods for teams to use and roll them out. They develop and advocate shared rituals. They've put together training videos promoting good collaboration hygiene and a library of meeting and workshop templates. They use surveys and polls to get feedback on how people are working together, which helps them improve and plan better collaboration.

Blake's role is now strategic. The new company org wouldn't function without the type of cross-functional connections he's built. He's taken what was originally an academic interest in new ways of working and literally made a career out of it.

How Can You Make Collaboration Work Better?

Blake is one of the first of his kind as a dedicated collaboration designer, but anyone running meetings can and should learn from the cutting-edge practices he and others like him are using to make team collaboration more intentional and productive.

Create a common collaboration space. First, you need to be deliberate about creating a common space for collaboration. This is about making sure everyone has a shared context and a shared medium of exchange. A collaboration designer doesn't even take for granted that people in the same room will be present to each other in the same collaboration space.

Make the space safe. The most important job of a collaboration designer is to create psychological safety for the team. Trust is foundational for collaboration to take hold, and the collaboration designer should initiate and host an explicit conversation about creative safety with the team.

Put diversity and inclusion into practice. Including and welcoming others is core to collaboration. Collaboration designers proactively seek contributions from the team by considering different work styles and preferences in the design of the collaboration because diversity must be baked in from the start.

Align on purpose. To focus a team's energy, there has to be a clear purpose. A collaboration designer orients collaboration to the team's mission. This is not just a clear agenda, which only gets at the what of collaboration. A well-defined purpose also speaks to the why. But it need not be delivered in a lengthy challenge statement. Collaboration designers are skilled at simply and directly sharing the intent behind the collaboration with the team before collaboration begins.

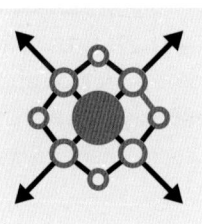

Build ongoing connections. Despite a hundred ways to communicate, people still feel disconnected from each other, from their teams, across departments, and with the larger enterprise and its goals. Collaboration design must include creating time and space for people to connect, particularly when chance meetings in a physical office are less and less common.

Guide problem-solving. Teams at work are expected to deliver business outcomes. Collaboration designers are proficient in selecting and implementing guided methods, or repeatable, structured approaches to direct collaboration, which help their teams solve problems and innovate together. Like exercising or building muscle, a team's ability to solve problems together gets better the more they work together and practice methodical approaches to how they collaborate.

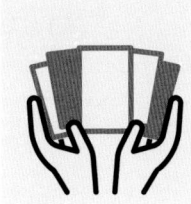

Roll out best practices. Collaboration designers identify methods that deliver the best results and create healthy teams. They gather and modify these best practices into templates and playbooks before rolling them out more broadly. Good curation skills are needed, too, for evaluating and updating methods of collaboration in the long term.

Assess collaboration quality. Collaboration designers reflect on and assess collaboration over time—at the individual, team, and organizational levels. Insights can come from a range of sources and can be informed by both quantitative metrics and qualitative feedback. Guidance from these insights about collaboration takes the guesswork out of teamwork.

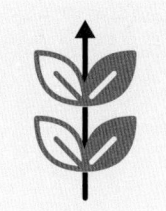

Ensure growth and development. In healthy teams, members should have the opportunity to learn and grow over time. Collaboration designers help each collaborator become more skilled at working together. Of particular importance is helping teams become more proficient in different modes of work, from in-person to remote to hybrid, as well as synchronous and asynchronous collaboration.

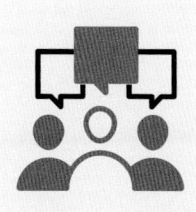

Make time to reflect. Regular reflection and introspection as a group helps the team continuously improve how they work together. To create a culture of collaboration, teams have to be able to talk about how they are collaborating.

Declaration of Interdependence

The healthiest, most effective teams we've observed make how they intend to work together explicit. Team charters or social agreements document how a team intends to interact.

A team charter is an agreement about how your particular group of teammates will best work together. These documents outline the essential elements of your team's communication and define a set of concepts and skills that will focus and guide you.

A typical charter documents several elements of a collaboration, including those shown in the following figure:

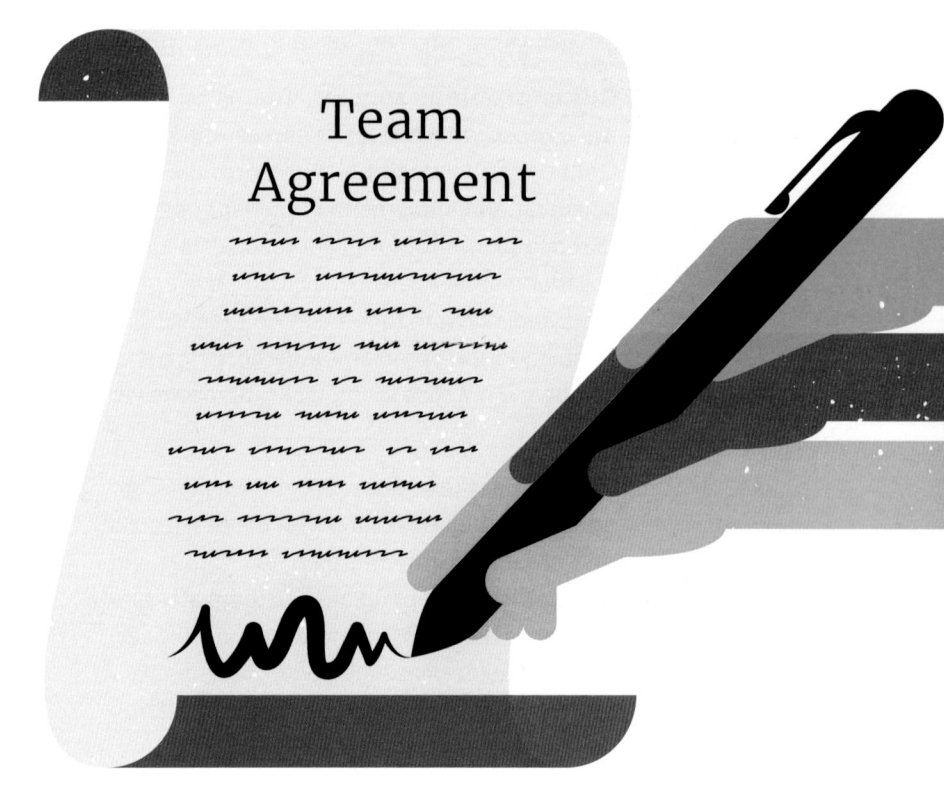

Team Charter

The best way to set up your team for success is to create a team charter: a set of concepts and skills that focus your team.

① Team Members
Who is on the team? Each team member lists two of their strengths and two of their weaknesses to help the team better understand each other.

	Name	Name	Name	Name
Strengths				
Weaknesses				

  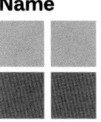

② Core Values
What do you care about? Discuss which shared values can help guide how you approach your work and how you collaborate with each other.

Brainstorm   **Consolidate**   **Refine**

 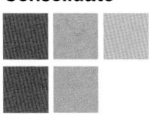

Value 1
Value 2
Value 3
...

③ Group Norms
How will you work? Establish a framework of ideals that you can expect each other to abide by.

Brainstorm   **Consolidate**   **Refine**

Norm 1
Norm 2
Norm 3
...

④ Roles
What roles are necessary? Determine the types of roles that will keep the team focused and drive productivity.

Brainstorm   **Consolidate**   **Refine**

Role 1
Role 2
Role 3
...

⑤ Metrics of Success
What does success look like to you? Consider how success can be measured beyond a letter grade or score.

Brainstorm   **Consolidate**   **Refine**

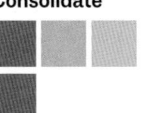

Metric 1
Metric 2
Metric 3
...

⑥ Standards of Quality
What are your standards for high-quality work? Think about the level of quality you deliver and expect from your teammates.

Brainstorm   **Consolidate**   **Refine**

 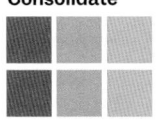

Standard 1
Standard 2
Standard 3
...

Understanding the Collaboration Experience

A focus on working arrangements and norms helps avoid confusion and miscommunication. We've seen detailed agreements that list tools the team will use, how to schedule meetings across time zones, what the expected turnaround times on answering questions from others should be, and more.

Sarah B. Nelson, chief design officer at Kyndryl, has coached teams and created team agreements for years. She told us:

> "A team agreement is about how a team intends to work together. It answers the key question about the type of environment they want to create for themselves beyond just what tools to use and when to communicate. Ultimately, it's a living tool that you can always come back to that describes what it should feel like to collaborate."

We've described the role of the collaboration designer as meeting teams where they are and helping them accomplish their goals and connect as individuals. But how can we find where our teams are? That is, how can we trace the experience of collaborating teams over time?

You've likely seen plenty of models that show ideas and innovations moving through cycles. Having worked closely with hundreds of teams across virtually every industry over the past decade, we've learned that teams cycle through phases too.

In fact, if we model the collaboration experience of a team over time, it looks like a journey through two distinct cycles: affective collaboration (how group members feel toward each other while interacting) and effective collaboration (how well they accomplish productive tasks). Each has its own phases that collide or coincide with the other as collaboration unfolds.

Model for a Collaboration Experience

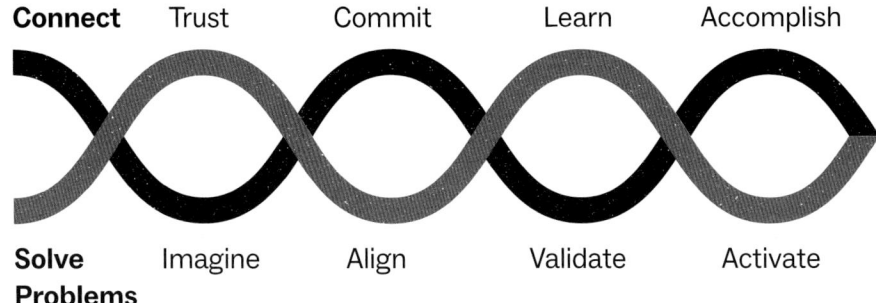

This is why the CEO of change agency Voltage Control, and one of our close partners, Douglas Ferguson, underscores that:

> "It's essential to design any organizational transformation with a foundation in psychological safety and relational awareness out of which to envision, prototype, practice, and reflect on the change over the longer-term for sustainable impact."

The discipline of collaboration design seeks to support and utilize these cycles. Balancing the two core elements of collaboration, skillful designers support a team throughout the quest to make something new.

Viewed from start to finish, collaborative intelligence is a journey filled with guided methods that are empathic and analytical, artistic and intellectual, playful and rigorous. Although there are many factors to consider—such as tools and technology for collaboration—at the core of the collaboration experience are these two jobs: **connecting** and **problem-solving**. Let's look at each in more detail.

Connecting

We know that in order to connect, teams need relational intelligence—the ability to develop interpersonal relationships among a group of people striving toward a common purpose. That connection is a mindset shift toward teams and teamwork that unfolds in four phases.

Trust. The members of a high-performing team must learn that others can respect individual contributions and will have their best interests in mind. In this stage, we cue collaboration activities that invite appropriate levels of vulnerability and encourage people to tune into each other. Through simple activities designed for connection, people on teams begin to build mutual understanding, appreciating that perfection is not required but mutual commitment to common ends is.

 **Commit.** With trust established, people can commit to the common pursuit of a goal. In the commitment stage, the team—implicitly or explicitly—agrees to lean into a shared pursuit of addressing and solving a challenge.

 **Learn.** A group grows together through experimentation, developing solutions, and investigating ways their work can gain momentum. At this stage, a team is focused on an objective, and it should be free to test, prototype, keep, and discard any ideas that have been brought to the table. This stage is notably generative. When teams are in this mode, their collective imaginations are unleashed and something new becomes possible.

 **Accomplish.** At this stage, the group has explored its best thinking and is converging on what, when, and how to execute. Group members take collective ownership of their output and greater appreciation of the diverse skill sets that made their new idea come to light. And because they've directly experienced group actualization, they're willing to imagine together again.

Of course, we recognize other models of team formation and connection that have influenced our thinking. An especially notable one is Bruce Tuckman's 1965 concept of these phases in team evolution[1]:

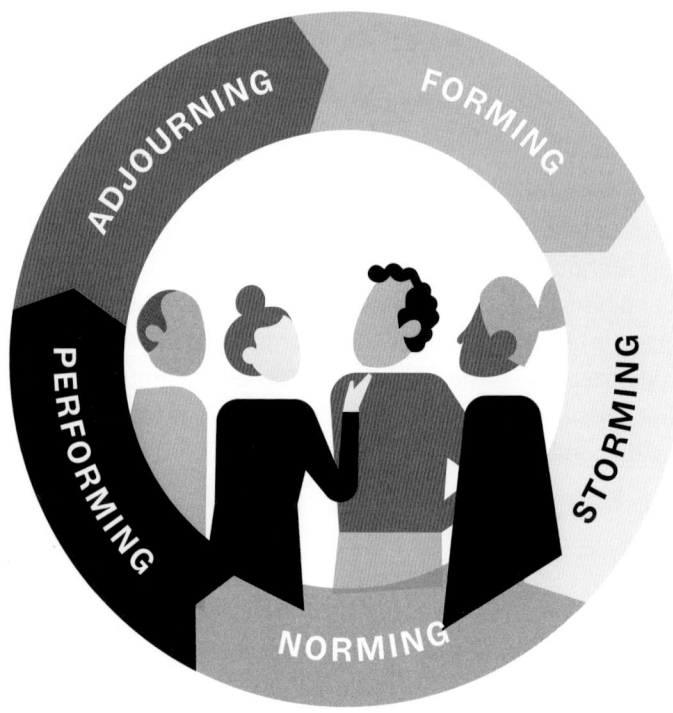

Forming. In this phase, the group not only comes together to form, it also develops relationship skills needed to work together.

Storming. Next, group members focus their attention and energy on the challenge at hand and begin to explore ways to solve it. Conflict and resistance may emerge as the team seeks to find common ground.

Norming. Group members eventually create harmony and strive to find effective ways of collaborating.

Performing. Actual task execution and problem-solving happens in this phase. Personal needs are put aside in favor of the success of the whole team.

Adjourning. A fifth phase was added to the model by Tuckman in 1977 to reflect completion of the challenge at hand. Celebrating accomplishment is key at this point in order to encourage and motivate members.

---

1   Bruce Tuckman, "Developmental sequence in small groups," Psychological Bulletin (1965)

Solving Problems

There are four arcs in our process: imagining, aligning, validating, and activating. These phases are found in similar form in any tried-and-true problem-solving process, and they also occur naturally in living systems, which diverge, explore, converge, exploit, and then start all over again.

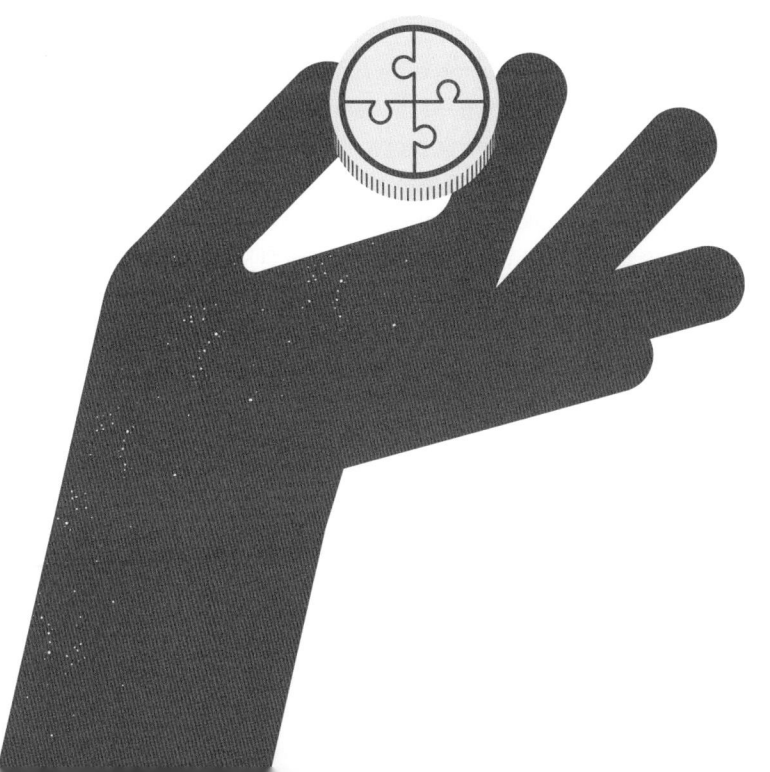

Imagine. Imagining is about teams coming together in collaborative spaces to freely externalize and visualize ideas, expanding and building on each other's thinking. In this phase, the focusing question of the team is "What might we do?"

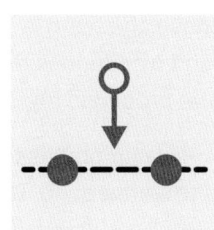
Align. Aligning involves the application of specialized methods and facilitators to help the team synthesize, prioritize, and consider making decisions. The clarifying question here is "How does it feel?" This inquiry helps teams discern if they're headed in the right general direction.

Validate. Validating is about teams being able to model, build, and execute experiments, identifying the candidates for solutions with the most promising potential. The unifying question in this phase is "How is it going?" This deceptively simple question is a reality- and a gut-check for the team in process.

Modeling Collaboration Experiences

Activate. Activating is where the rubber hits the road. This phase is when ideas are operationalized through planning, execution, and pipelining into core business systems and workflows. The pointed question here is "What are we making?" In this phase, the team is in builder mode. The energy and attention is on the manifestation of the ideas and solutions they've produced together over the cycle.

The framework of this problem-solving process is linear, but we purposely make room for activities to shift around. This is where the craft of collaboration design shines. Collaboration design know-how makes it possible to adjust dynamically while nurturing a healthy exchange within the group.

Less of a prescription or a rigid path, our model of the collaborative experience weaves the most potent forces of collaboration design—connecting with each other through relational intelligence and solving challenges together—to reflect the nonlinear reality of deep group work while also elevating it.

Collaboration design isn't just about improving meetings that happen in real time. It's also about the behaviors and activities that happen in between live interactions. And it's about the development of teamwork, belonging, and accomplishment over time, as well. Our model of collaboration integrates all of these elements.

At the simplest level, you can think of any collaboration experiences as having a beginning, middle, and end.

The core of this model is problem-solving.

This kind of problem-solving is perhaps the most intensely collective point in the model: It's where the team must truly collaborate at the same time. Still, at its opening, problem-solving is characterized by divergence, as the team engages in explorations, spreading out in search of a solution. This is followed by the group converging as a team to make decisions. Over time, this process is shaped like an emerald (Figure A on page 51), with work opening out (as our friends Dave Gray, Sunni Brown, and James Macanufo put it in *Gamestorming*) from a starting point and then coming together to close in on a solution.

Figure A

Figure B

At the same time, collaboration design recognizes that any team problem-solving must be connected to development of the team and the relationships within the group. Being deliberate about the relational layer here means taking time to connect before problem-soving and reflect together afterward (Figure B at right).

But it's not only the synchronous collaboration behaviors that matter. While spending time together, whether in-person or remote, is important, the real power in collaboration design lies in managing individual asynchronous work. This happens both before and after real-time interactions (Figure C at right). Zooming out, the model starts to become more complete.

Figure C

Together Time

Open
Problem

Close
Solution

EXPLORE

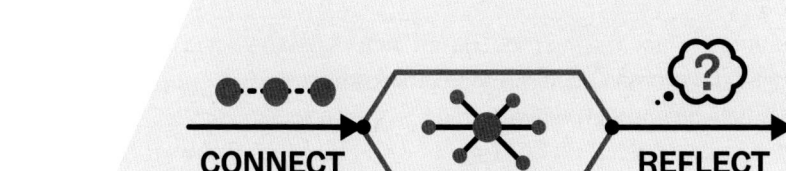

CONNECT

EXPLORE

REFLECT

Alone Time

Together Time

Alone Time

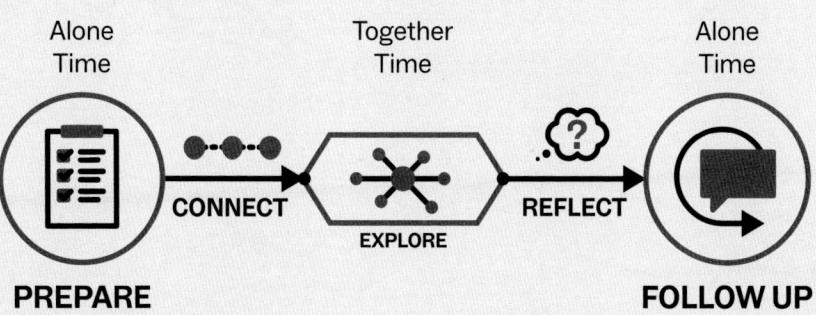

PREPARE

CONNECT

EXPLORE

REFLECT

FOLLOW UP

Zooming out even further, we can look at how the collaborative behaviors of the group improve over time. This includes assessing how the group is performing by using both quantitative and qualitative insights.

At this level, we see that the overall design of collaboration is nested and iterative. Teamwork is situated in the context of other projects and ongoing work. One interaction might be part of a continuum of arcs within larger loops of work. Collaboration design is ultimately about understanding the intent of the collaboration and placing it in a broader scope, and creating experiences that both connect team members and drive business outcomes.

Here's the best part about the fact that this model is not linear: It means you can start anywhere at any time. Over time, relationships build and teams improve their ability to problem-solve.

In other words, the best time to start being more intentional about collaboration is right now. Take the next meeting you have coming up. Introduce a new practice, such as a brief check-in or warm-up. See how it goes, and iterate from there. Then start introducing more and more collaboration methods. You'll soon see that there's no shortage of these practices—and ways to combine them.

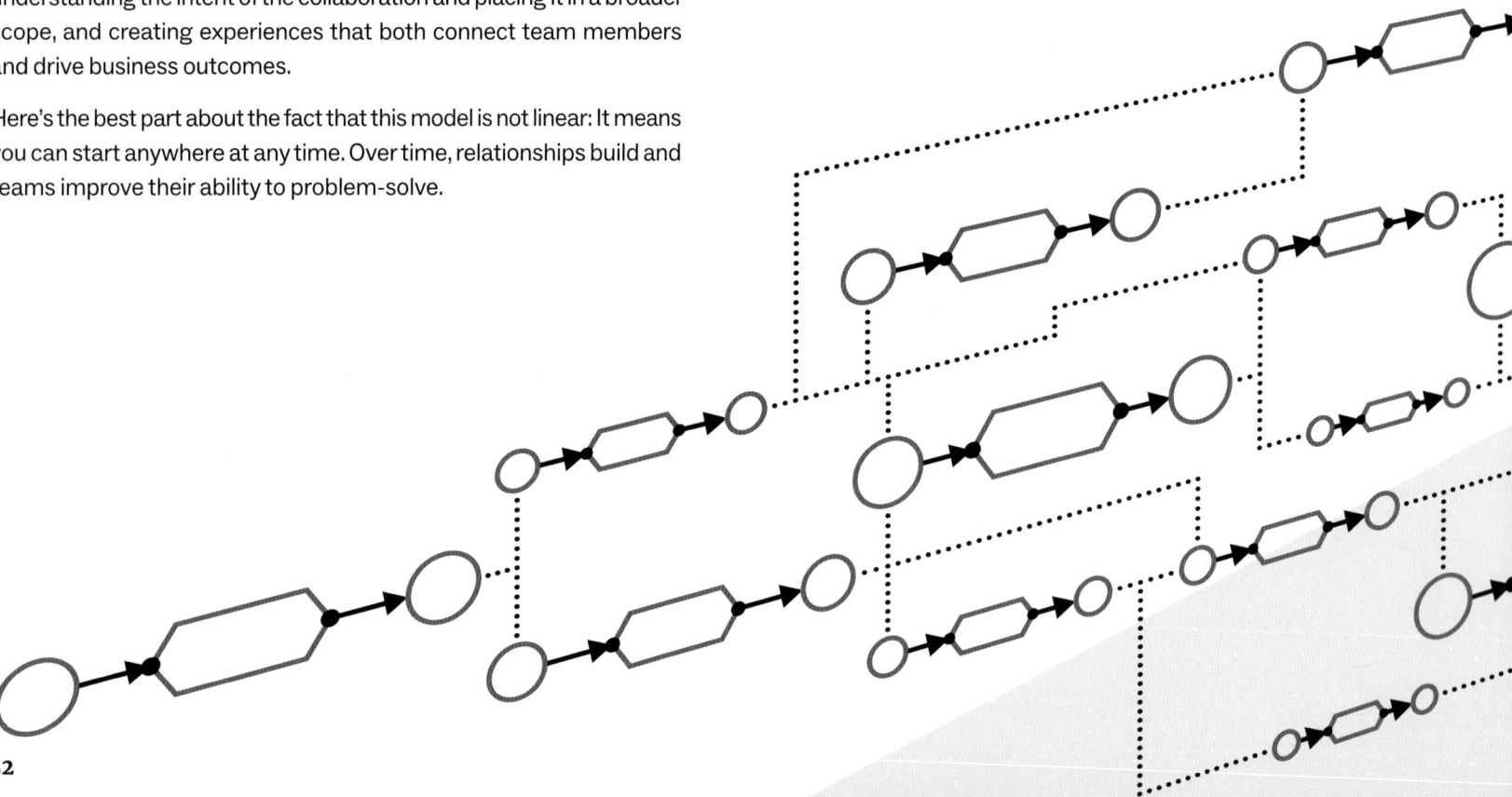

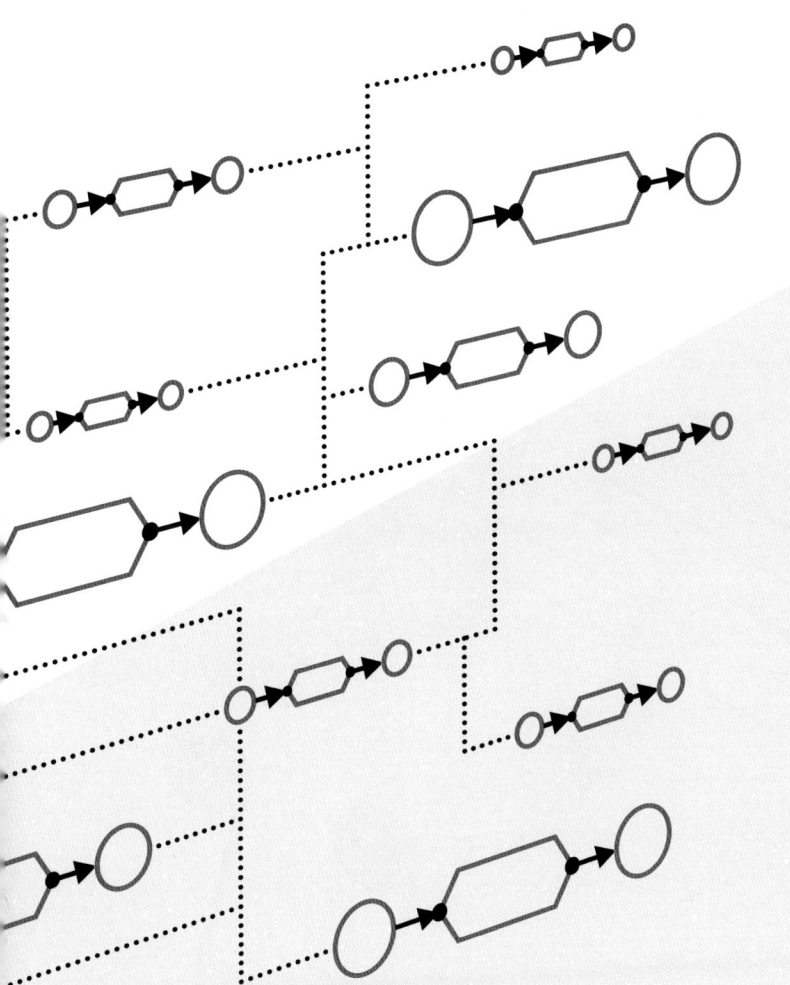

Recommended Reading

Priya Parker, *The Art of Gathering* (2018)

Parker's detailed investigation of how people meet starts with the assumption that social connections and interpersonal relationships are of paramount importance. This volume is one of the best in terms of understanding how people come together

Daniel Stillman, *Good Talk* (2020)

This guide to having better conversations is broken into bite-sized chunks of practical insight that can be applied immediately. Stillman's Conversations OS presents nine core facets of conservations. Ultimately, this book is about how human beings interact with each other and how to design better interactions.

Michael Schrage, *Shared Minds* (1990)

Ahead of its time and very prescient, Schrage's *Shared Minds* offers detailed theories and principles of collaboration, as well as a wealth of practical advice. His chapter on "Collaboration Design Themes" is particularly relevant.

Find more online at
www.collaborativeintelligence.com

Chapter 4

Collaboration Methods

Playbooks for Working Together

In 1959, Miles Davis entered the studio to record what would become the best-selling, most popular jazz recording of all time: *Kind of Blue*. Even if you don't like mainstream jazz, you'll probably appreciate this album. The songs are approachable, the band sounds great, and every solo is a home run.

Davis was known for forcing his musicians to be spontaneous, so there were no rehearsals for this recording date. In fact, he gave the musicians the music to be recorded only as they entered the studio. Astoundingly, with only one exception, the first complete take of each tune for *Kind of Blue* was the one that got pressed on the album. In other words, they nailed it on the first try.

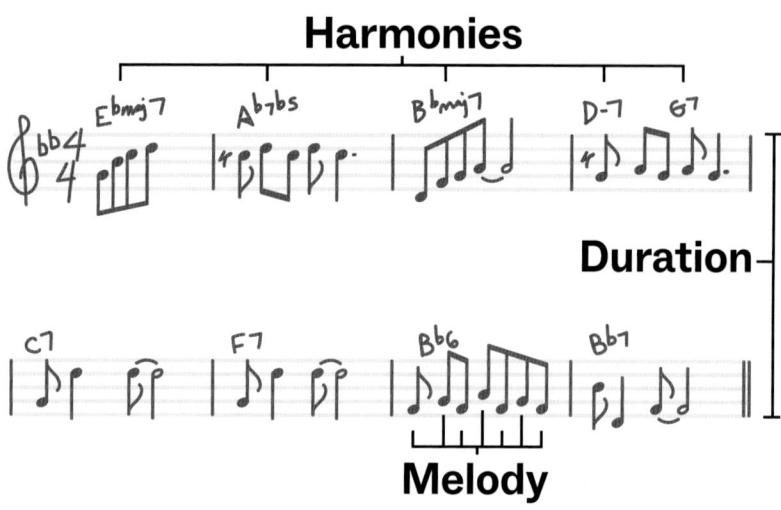

How is it possible for a group to come together and spontaneously create such a great work of art? What are the tools that allow for this type of exceptional collaboration? What can we learn from this group?

One of the keys to success in mainstream jazz improvisation is structure. That's right, contrary to popular belief, jazz musicians are not just making things up when they improvise. Instead, the players are well organized and follow common rules of engagement.

In particular, a "lead sheet" in jazz outlines the form of a tune. The lead sheet provides only three pieces of information: the **melody**, the **harmonies**, and the **duration**. That's it—everything all jazz musicians need to be able to perform as a group. The rest is made up on the fly, or "faked," as they say. In fact, a collection of lead sheets in jazz is called a "fake book."

Free jazz contrasts this approach. In free jazz, the improvisation is more total, even including the underlying form. There are no predetermined structures to follow. The result, to the average listener, is often abstract and obtuse. And without highly trained musicians, the music can fall apart quickly.

Now consider how your teams collaborate at work: Are you following the same lead sheet, or are you making up the form as you go? It turns out that much of workplace collaboration is improvised on the fly. Sure, we might have a meeting agenda, but an agenda is just a list of topics that doesn't clarify what the activities will look like. The structure of how we interact, decide, and make sense as a group is largely improvised.

Like free jazz, the results of meetings are often abstract, even chaotic, leaving people unclear, unfocused, and frustrated. We've all experienced the symptoms of bad meetings:

- A few people dominate the conversations

- Boring presentations lull participants to sleep

- Politics are played out in real time

- A lack of closure and actionable outcomes

- The result is all talk—and no artifacts or materials to show for it

Guided Autonomy

A common problem in team collaboration is what we call "blank canvas paralysis": the group convenes with no plan on how to collaborate. Imagine a team standing in front of a whiteboard asking, "Now what?" Without a plan, the rules of engagement are improvised, often resulting in poor collaboration.

With collaboration methods, getting from point A to point B doesn't have to be a mystery each time. And they work without constraining creativity or the freedom to think outside of the box; instead, methods often have a liberating effect, giving teams the latitude to act and allowing their collective imagination to flourish.

Joe Lalley, founder of Joe Lalley Experience Design, told us:

> "Structured collaboration methods give you a way to bring your team together to focus on a problem area. You don't have to guess or improvise your way through the process to reach a conclusion or a decision—the method gets you there together."

But what if your teams, instead, were playing from the same page? What if instead of having an agenda and winging it, they used a proven set of methods to guide and direct collaboration? What if everyone understood the basic structure so that they could come in and play well together?

There's actually a wealth of these structures. We call them "guided methods." They're simple to follow, easy to implement and customize, and deliver better results each time you put them to work. Best of all, they can supercharge your teams' time collaborating together, whether in-person or remote and whether synchronously or asynchronously.

What collaboration practices need the most improvement in your organization? How might introducing guided methods for deeper connections and better problem-solving benefit your teams? What's one small thing you can try immediately to get more intentional about collaboration in your organization?

The Games Teams Play

Imagine playing a game with no rules. It wouldn't be fun, would it? It turns out that much of the enjoyment we get while playing comes from an agreed set of guidelines. When everyone knows how the rules work, the participation and involvement increase, and a group can really connect and be creative.

Collaboration methods provide "rules of engagement" for collaboration and allow team members to work together on equal footing, generating better results. And at the same time, methods make work more playful.

Collaboration methods, broadly defined, include any and all exercises, activities, games, frameworks, and techniques that thoughtfully direct team interaction. Think of them like sheet music for team collaboration: They provide a set of rules to follow and allow for creative freedom at the same time.

There are thousands of collaboration methods from various fields with many examples to point to. In each case, their function is the same: to make collaboration explicit and deliberate. Teams don't have to guess or react; they can all be on the same page.

Take, for example, the rituals from Agile practice, an approach for developing software that structures how teams priorities and focus on small chunks at a time. Formal methodologies like Scrum guide teams to collaborate in a very intentional way. Exercises such as "planning poker"

simulate a game of cards, where participants have effort points to "bet" like chips in a round of poker. It literally brings game-like interactions into solving problems as a team.

Then there's Hills, a collaboration method pioneered at IBM. It's a simple guided method to get a project team to identify and agree on a measurable problem statement. A Hill consists of three elements:

Who. The customers you're targeting to serve

What. The need they're trying to meet

Wow. How you'll differentiate from competitors by "wow-ing" customers

IBM's Hills method guides team collaboration toward a shared mission state-ment for any effort.

The Business Model Canvas, developed by Alexander Osterwalder and the team at Strategyzer.

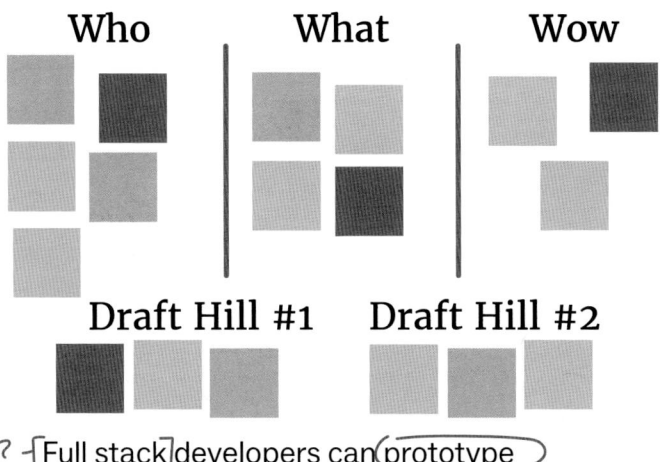

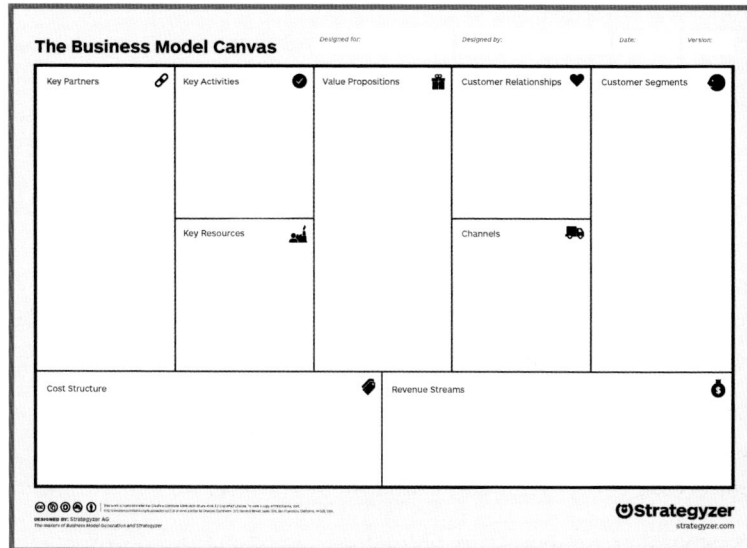

The output of the exercise is a Hill statement:

"A sales leader can assemble a response team in under 24 hours without management involvement."

"It should take no more than 13 minutes for a developer to build and run an app using third-party APIs."

Even complex problems, like determining business strategy, can benefit from a methodical approach. For example, the Business Model Canvas, developed by Alexander Osterwalder and the team at Strategyzer, is a collaboration tool for exploring different possible business models. Nine boxes represent the core elements of any business model, and an entire team fills them out one by one. This process is meant to ensure not only that all aspects of the business have been discussed, but also that everyone has been able to contribute on an equal footing.

Methods like these are a key tool for collaboration designers to guide team collaboration in a very intentional way. They are your opportunity to make collaboration more deliberate. What's more, collaboration methods create fun and playful shared experiences. It's the moments we play together that really instill a sense of team connectedness and give rise to team empowerment, psychological safety, and strong relationships.

Structures and Patterns

The best collaboration methods share some basic common benefits, including:

- Helping include more voices for a diversity of perspectives

- Promoting imagination and creativity

- Making it easier to spot new patterns and opportunities

- Drawing out better results

- Saving time

Henri Lipmanowicz and Keith McCandless, the authors of *The Surprising Power of Liberating Structures*, use the term "microstructures" to describe the rituals and habits that shape the way we work with others:

> "Consciously or not, microstructures are the way you organize all your routine interactions. They guide and control how groups work together. They shape your conversations and meetings."[1]

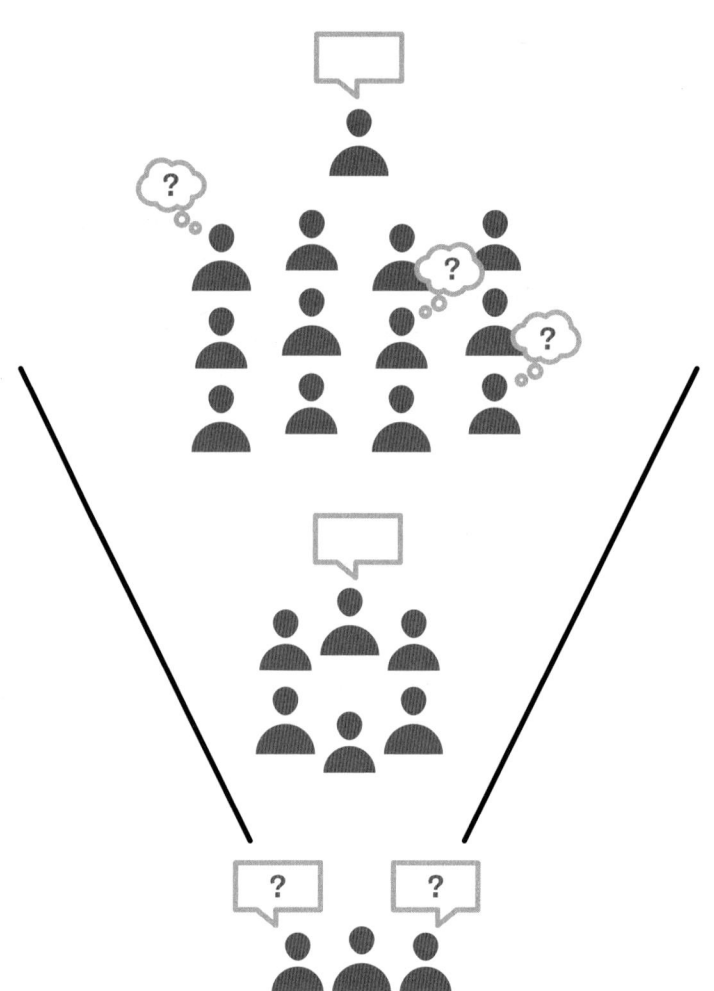

---

1   Microstructures & Design Elements, Liberating Structures, https://www.liberatingstructures.com/design-elements/.

On their own, these organizing patterns, however, typically don't allow for broad participation and for creativity to flourish. And bad habits of collaboration are all too common, like a few voices dominating conversations and not allowing for diverse perspectives to be heard. However, the authors offer a series of what they call "liberating structures." These are methods specifically designed to shape collaboration in a way that "liberates" input from the whole group.

For instance, one of their collaboration methods is called "1-2-4-All." It's simple to use, and fits many different situations. The instructions are right in the title:

- First, participants reflect individually on the topic at hand (1 minute)

- Next, they get into pairs to share and compare each others thoughts (2 minutes)

- Then, groups of four share reflections and improve on their ideas together (2 minutes)

- Finally, the whole group re-convenes and shares concepts with everyone (3 minutes)

One of the beauties of liberating structures is that they are largely self-facilitating. That is, they are not only easy to use and approachable,

they don't necessarily require a dedicated facilitator to put into action. Teams can agree to use liberating structures, and for the most part, put them into use right away.

The liberating structures framework consists of 33 methods, each representing a tiny shift in how we meet and relate to each other. Other examples include:

Generative Relationships. This technique helps a group understand how they work together. Participants first assess their team in terms of four attributes (Separateness, Tuning, Action, and Reason—or STAR) and then assemble a list of action steps to improve collaboration.

Heard, Seen, Respected (HSR). Teams can actively practice listening and having empathy for each other. Each person shares a story about NOT being heard, seen, or respected. The others listen and reflect on the patterns in the stories and what can be done to improve collaboration. HSR is particularly good for building trust and strengthening relational intelligence in a team.

TRIZ. This method is based on a single, foundational question: "What must we stop doing to make progress on our deepest purpose?" The team makes a collective list to discuss, and the result is often fun yet courageous conversations.

Of course, there are other sources of collaboration patterns as well. One of the best is the collection of activities gathered by Dave Gray, Sunni Brown, and James Macanufo in their book *Gamestorming*. Kursat Ozenc and Margaret Hagan also provide a range of techniques to improve collaboration in *Rituals for Work*. And one of our favorites is Hyper Island Toolbox, available for free online (*https://toolbox.hyperisland.com/*). The list goes on and on.

But don't be overwhelmed: A limited set of methods is all that's needed for your team to collaborate better. Your first step to using collaboration methods is adding one simple technique to your team interaction. Just know that there are many more resources out there that help you explore and adapt methods over time.

The net effect will be that the overall team-member experience is improved. People become more engaged and are more likely to connect with each other when their work is guided with methods. Imagine every person and every team having a better experience and working more effectively. Just a small nudge in the right direction can have a dramatic effect on driving business results, which in turn, creates real ROI for your organization.

Combining Methods

You might be wondering, how you can get hundreds or thousands of people in an organization to learn and remember all these methods. It may seem exhausting at first glance.

One way to accelerate the adoption of these methods is to leverage existing frameworks. The LUMA system, for instance, helps teams find the right techniques to use for innovation by guiding collaboration designers in a structured way. LUMA has distilled their portfolio down to 36 of the most effective tools for innovation—the majority of them in common use. You don't need to know them all right away—a handful of them are enough to get started.

The LUMA system is organized into three key design skills: looking, understanding, and making.

Looking. Successful innovation requires curiosity and empathy for the people you serve. This begins and ends with the observation of people. The methods in the category reflect the careful investigation of the human problems you target and innovate around.

Understanding. Innovators must carefully understand the problems they want to solve with critical thinking and rigorous problem framing. Methods in the understanding category help teams do this together in a structured, repeatable way.

Making. Ideas alone have no value. Successful teams put their concepts into action by first representing ideas and then bringing them to life. Imagination, visual representation, and frequent iteration are required to make artifacts that embody your innovation, even in the earliest stages.

Each of these categories is divided into three subcategories, and each subcategory contains four innovation tools. This hierarchical model makes it much easier to identify the tools you need and then put them to use.

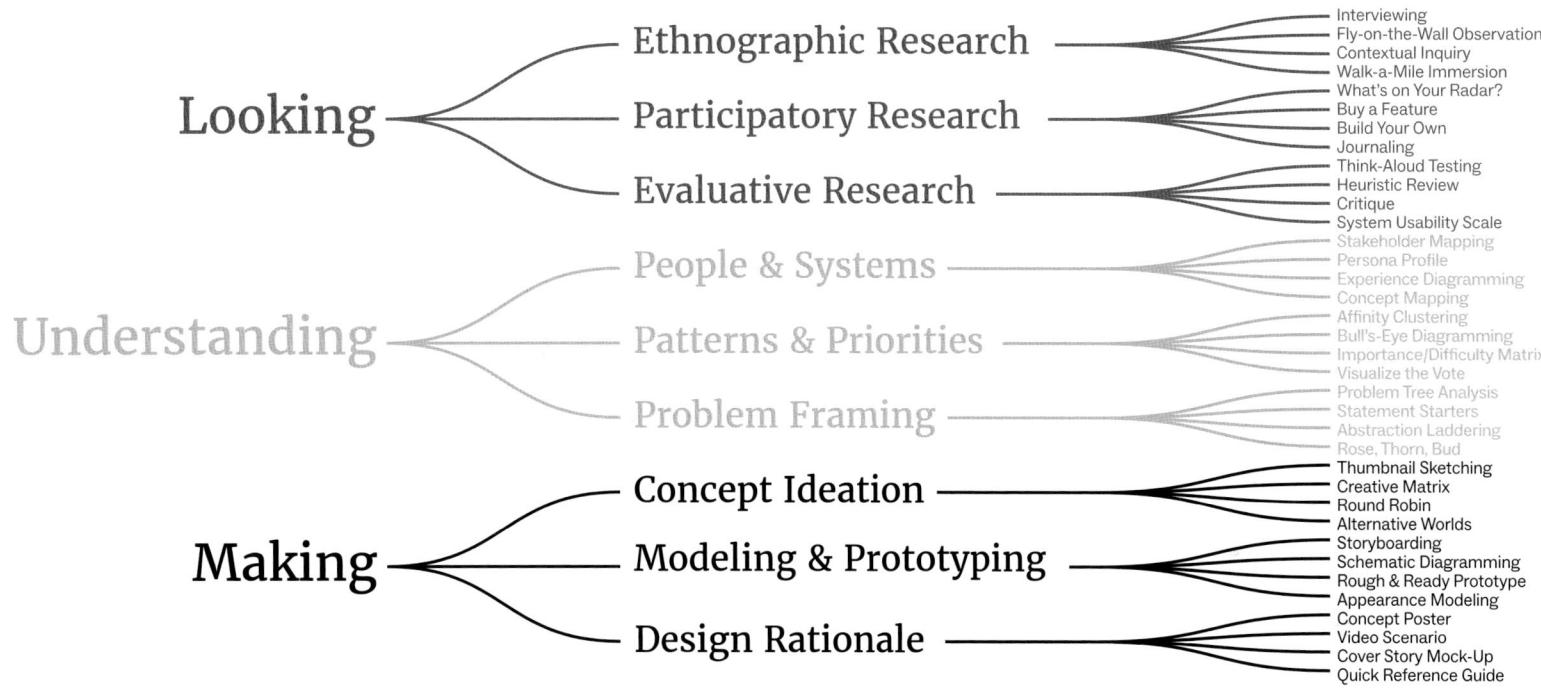

Looking
- Ethnographic Research
  - Interviewing
  - Fly-on-the-Wall Observation
  - Contextual Inquiry
  - Walk-a-Mile Immersion
- Participatory Research
  - What's on Your Radar?
  - Buy a Feature
  - Build Your Own
  - Journaling
- Evaluative Research
  - Think-Aloud Testing
  - Heuristic Review
  - Critique
  - System Usability Scale

Understanding
- People & Systems
  - Stakeholder Mapping
  - Persona Profile
  - Experience Diagramming
  - Concept Mapping
- Patterns & Priorities
  - Affinity Clustering
  - Bull's-Eye Diagramming
  - Importance/Difficulty Matrix
  - Visualize the Vote
- Problem Framing
  - Problem Tree Analysis
  - Statement Starters
  - Abstraction Laddering
  - Rose, Thorn, Bud

Making
- Concept Ideation
  - Thumbnail Sketching
  - Creative Matrix
  - Round Robin
  - Alternative Worlds
- Modeling & Prototyping
  - Storyboarding
  - Schematic Diagramming
  - Rough & Ready Prototype
  - Appearance Modeling
- Design Rationale
  - Concept Poster
  - Video Scenario
  - Cover Story Mock-Up
  - Quick Reference Guide

https://hbr.org/2014/01/a-taxonomy-of-innovation

The LUMA System

Methods in the LUMA system can be combined and recombined into what are called recipes. In fact, this is its real power. These suggested sequences of individual exercises get the whole team on a path to a solution.

For instance, if a team has challenges **aligning on near-term priorities**, there's a recipe that will get them on the same page. It consists of four steps that include input from the whole team:

1. **"Rose, Thorn, Bud"** is an exercise that allows the team to reflect on the topic at hand from multiple perspectives.

2. **"Affinity Clustering"** helps the team find patterns in its reflections.

3. **"Visualize the Vote"** allows team members to highlight clusters that are most important to them individually and then find common patterns across the team.

4. **"Importance Difficulty Matrix"** fosters a discussion around the concepts they agree to move forward with first.

Align a team on near-term priorities

Solicit opinions across a team in order to identify themes and transform them into a shared plan of action.

 Rose, Thorn, Bud

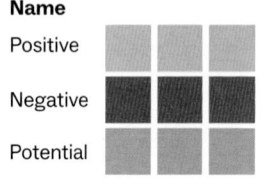

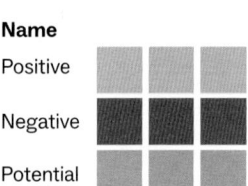

 Affinity Clustering

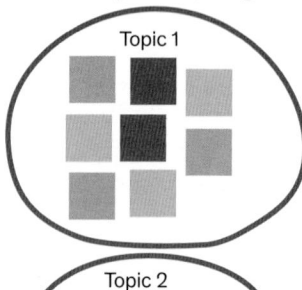

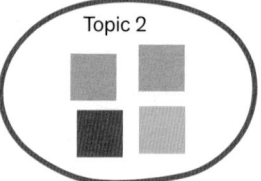

 Visualize the Vote

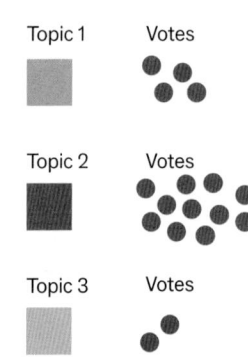

 Importance Difficulty Matrix

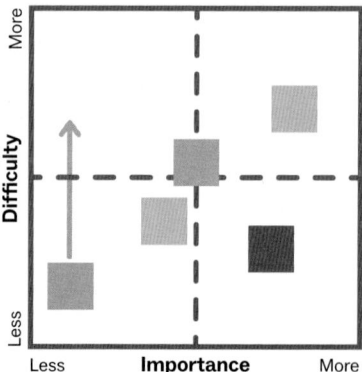

There are also recipes for strengthening the relational intelligence of a group. A recipe that we've found particularly effective helps teams gain empathy for someone else by learning about their life experiences. There are four steps to this recipe:

1. **Interviewing.** Learn about someone using interviews. Create an interview guide and talk to someone who self-identifies in a way that is different from you.

2. **Experience Diagramming.** Create a "life line" by visually depicting the emotional experience of your interviewee to get a sense of it over time.

3. **Rose, Thorn, Bud.** Together, visually codify the Experience Diagram so that you can see where positives, negatives, and opportunities lie.

4. **Alternative worlds.** Leverage each other's different perspectives to help generate fresh ideas and shared understanding.

Gain Empathy for Someone Else by Learning about Their Life Experiences

Interviewing

Protocol   Interview   Notes

Experience Diagramming

Positive Aspects

Time

Negative Aspects

Rose, Thorn, Bud

Name

Positive

Negative

Potential

Name

Positive

Negative

Potential

Alternative Worlds

Notes

But there's more to LUMA than just a way to organize methods. Even the name is meant as a mnemonic for solving problems together—a profound reminder of the fundamental behaviors at the root of effective collaboration: It calls for us to **look** carefully, **understand** deeply, **make** resourcefully, and **adapt** accordingly.

Taken together, these form the LUMA principle, which summarizes key actions and attitudes that need to be adopted—both individually and collectively. It's also a sequential process and a dynamic way of operating, in which various mixtures of looking, understanding, and making activities inform adaptive change.

Similar principles and lines of thinking can be found in other organizations. IBM is one of the more successful examples of leveraging the method

of design thinking to affect organizational changes. Their Enterprise Design Thinking (EDT) program was built and rolled out over a decade.

Similar to LUMA, EDT offers a complete design thinking toolkit and activation plan. It was originally intended for internal use at IBM, but more recently, they've made it available to the general public and have started consulting clients.

Whether you develop your own set of playbooks, like IBM has done with EDT, or rely on a pre-existing system, finding unique and appropriate ways to combine methods helps educate and scale across teams within an organization.

Making Collaboration Methods an Everyday Practice

Change rarely happens from the top down only; lasting transformation tends to work from the bottom up. Thus, in knowledge work, guided methods help activate better collaboration, interaction by interaction, on the ground level.

Like learning an instrument, the more you play the better you get. You have to break down things into smaller parts. You have to practice. This is a muscle you have to build within and across teams over time.

At first, your aim in applying collaboration methods should simply be to internalize the rules of play. Things might even be awkward at the outset, but once everyone on a team knows the steps and the process, it becomes fluid.

For example, you might want to build more empathy by using a team warm-up before each meeting. We've found that using a short prompt to begin each interaction can help getting to know your teammates on a personal level. Try something like "What was your first job?" or "What's your favorite bad movie?"

The use of any one guided method like this by itself might seem inconsequential. But over time, as you add and by adding more and more, you'll be able to affect your team's culture in a deliberate way.

The idea is to create a series of "tiny habits," a behavior change approach pioneered by BJ Fogg. His research shows that transformation happens best by taking baby steps. Tiny habits work by first finding a trigger event and then attaching the new behavior to it.

Fogg recommends using this statement to get started:

After I _trigger_, I will _new habit_.

For example, if you want to build better habits around dental hygiene, you might try doing this: After I brush my teeth, I'll floss just one tooth. From there you'd move to two teeth, three teeth, and so on. Eventually flossing all of your teeth after you brush becomes an effortless, almost unconscious action.

This approach to behavior design is proven to work for several reasons. The most important of them is time. Making sweeping, team-wide change takes a lot of effort and time. Just thinking of all of the materials to create and training to deliver for a team to change all at once can crush initiatives. There's something daunting about making large changes that sets them up for failure. Instead, taking incremental steps helps overcome inertia in a realistic way.

Setting up a series of tiny habits your team can practice to improve how they collaborate is a small, achievable goal. It's the kind of change that adds up to transformation over time. And simple guided methods are modular enough that you can start right now—tomorrow in your next team meeting, for instance. With practice, the team will improve over time, cultivating for collaboration each time they gather.

Meta, for instance, broke down activities for team collaboration into manageable chunks in its Facebook Think Kit toolkit for rapid collaboration, ideation, and problem-solving across teams. It's a series of exercises rooted in design thinking and customer-centric methods. Each activity has simple instructions and worksheets to help teams follow along visually.

Exercises can be used on their own or combined with "suggested pairings" to achieve goals. The Think Kit allows teams to make creative thinking a habit, one exercise at a time—from setting a North Star together to running a pre-mortem to creating a storyboard.

Now it's your turn to try it with your team. Start small by introducing just one new activity to bring about change. For instance, if you want to make sure certain voices don't always dominate and that everyone has a chance to speak, you might introduce "popcorning" as a way to take turns. With this method, the last person to speak picks the next, until everyone has had a chance. This helps establish a safe environment where everyone's input is valued.

Find the prompt to invoke popcorning and make a statement around it, for example, "After we initiate feedback gathering in a meeting, we'll use popcorning to regulate turn taking."

Repeat that behavior until it feels natural for your team

2×2 Prioritization Matrix

Overview

2×2 matrixes provide a visual way for teams to build shared understanding and make collective decisions for moving ideas forward. Use this activity to evaluate and prioritize new ideas, strategic directions, ideal target audience, and more.

Gather Your Ideas

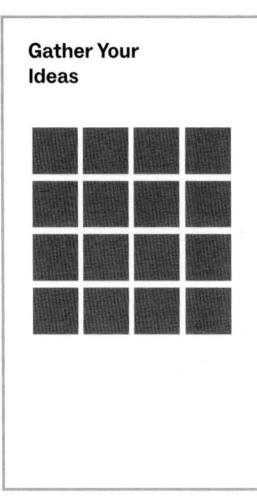

Let's get started

1 Gather your ideas.

2 Determine an initial set of criteria for sorting and prioritizing.

3 Round 1 — Sort, share and discuss.

4 Round 2 — Re-sort along even more relevant criteria.

5 Reflection and next steps.

Criteria & Considerations

ROUND 1

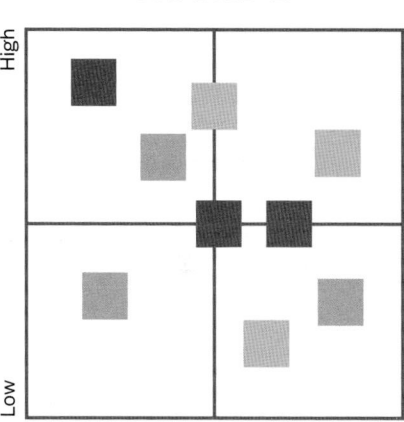

ROUND 2

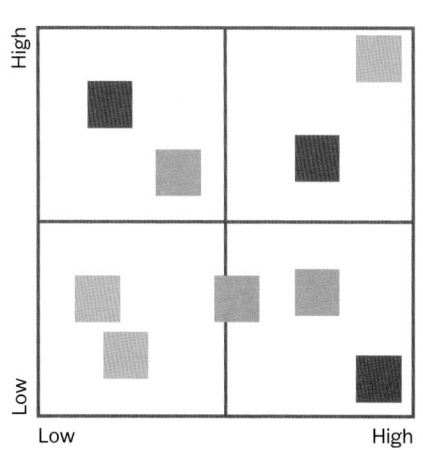

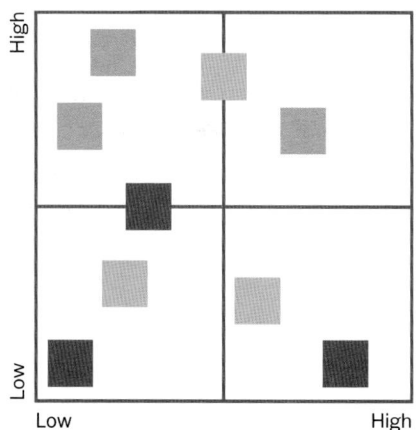

Then introduce another practice that you want to adopt. This might be something like adding short reflections at the end of each meeting using three categories of input in the format "I liked..., I wish..., I wonder..." as taught at the Stanford dSchool. Soon you'll have whole recipes of methods.

Finally, keep in mind that expert collaboration designers are available to guide the habit building. Good collaboration design goes beyond one-off interactions and helps teams accumulate successful practices over time.

Once you no longer have to think about adding methods, you'll start customizing them. Every team is different, and your playbooks need to be relevant and appropriate to your context. Soon, you'll be jamming from your own lead sheets.

Recommended Reading

**Henri Lipmanowicz and Keith McCandless,
*The Surprising Power of Liberating
Structures* (2013)**

This book is probably the best resource on collaboration methods out there. The authors provide a range of theory and background material before presenting their 33 methods, which are also available at www.liberatingstructures.com.

BJ Fogg, *Tiny Habits* (2020)

A professor at Stanford, Fogg has a broad reputation for having some of the best research on how habits form. The title of this book is also the punchline: start small and make changes incrementally. See also his accompanying website, www.tinyhabits.com, where you can try out a behavior yourself with his online tools.

LUMA Institute, *Innovating for People* (2012)

This handbook of human-centered design methods forms a great foundation for collaboration design. The founders of LUMA carefully selected 36 of the most effective methods that are also easy to teach, each explained here with enough detail to

run them on your own. See also the article in the *Harvard Business Review* from 2014 "Taxonomy of Innovation" in which LUMA explains their hierarchy of methods.

**Dave Gray, Sunni Brown, and James Macanufo,
Gamestorming (2010)**

This is a timeless classic that facilitators can use over and over again to plan meetings, workshops, and more. It's effectively a collection of exercises and activities that you can run to engage teams in various ways. The introduction provides a particularly good explanation of meeting shapes and how to design the overall experience.

Kursat Ozenc and Margaret Hagan, *Rituals For Work* (2019)

Based on research and team psychology, the authors present 50 rituals that you can use right away to strengthen your collaboration habits. See also the follow up book *Rituals for Virtual Meetings* (2020; with Glenn Fajardo) with a collection of remote-friendly rituals.

Find more online at
www.collaborativeintelligence.com

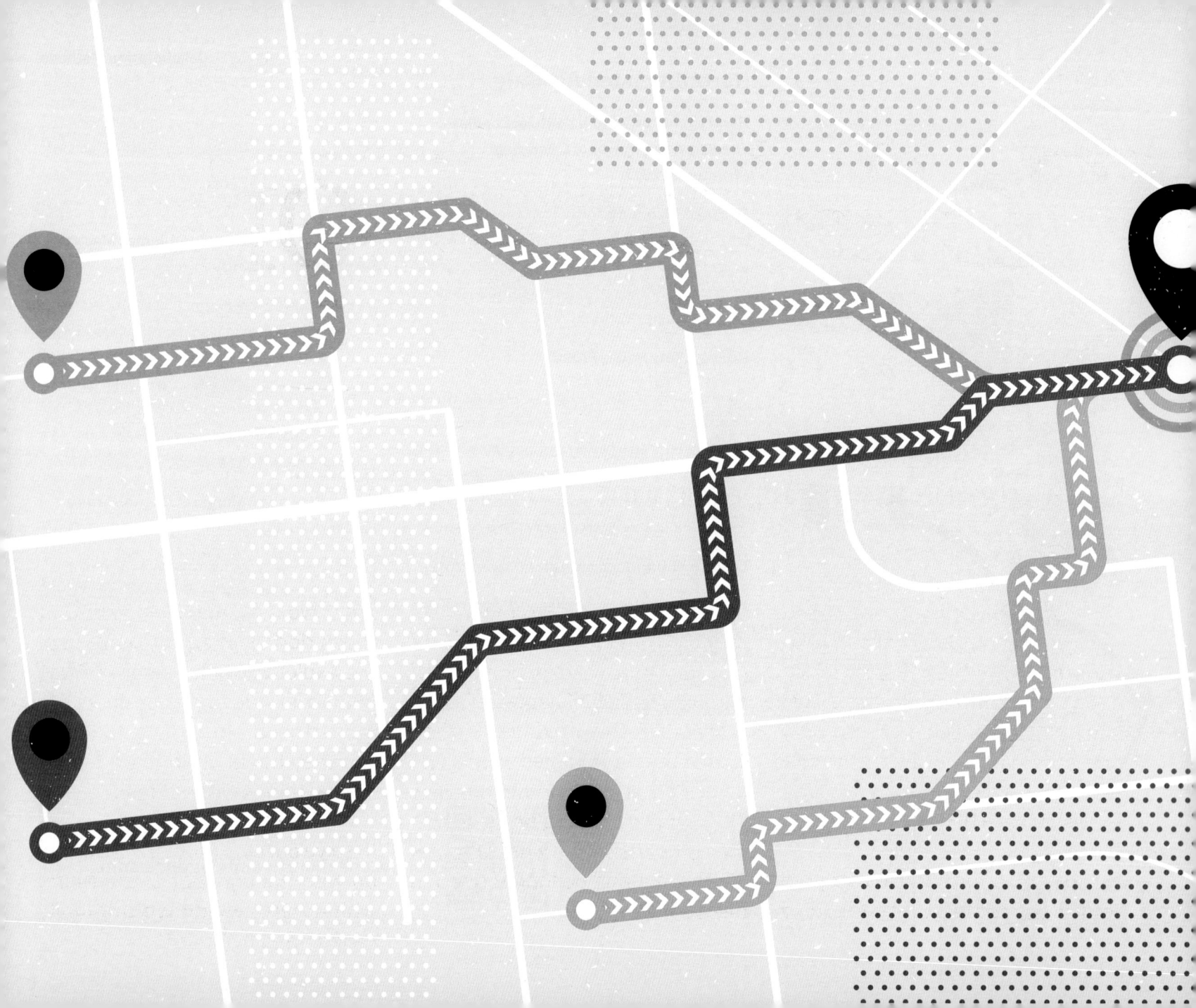

Chapter 5

Collaboration Spaces

Creating the Ideal Environment

I n 2005, I (Mariano) co-founded a small company called Three Melons, which focused on creating online games. After launching an online hit called Bola and spending some time on the market, we were lucky to be acquired by Disney in 2010.

No longer a small start-up, we found ourselves collaborating between Buenos Aires (our home city), Mountain View, and Los Angeles. Now, we experienced the passive cognitive style of slide decks first-hand: Our new colleagues leaned back and judged each bullet point. Rather than contributing new ideas and improving on what was there, they assumed what they saw was "done" and no longer open to discussion.

What we saw, however, was that slides don't invite participation or the exploration of concepts. They tend to lull audiences to sleep. We wanted people to participate, to feel like they could change and even "break" things without fear.

To solve our own problem, we came up with the concept of the Mural whiteboard, which we originally called "Medley Board."

Medley Board was a concept for a two-dimensional online environment that allowed participants to visualize their thoughts and ideas in a variety of ways. It made use of color and shapes and different formats, and participants could move around freely on a shared whiteboard. It was our always-on, always-available resource for teams, a space that could be adapted to meet the needs of our organization and our imagination.

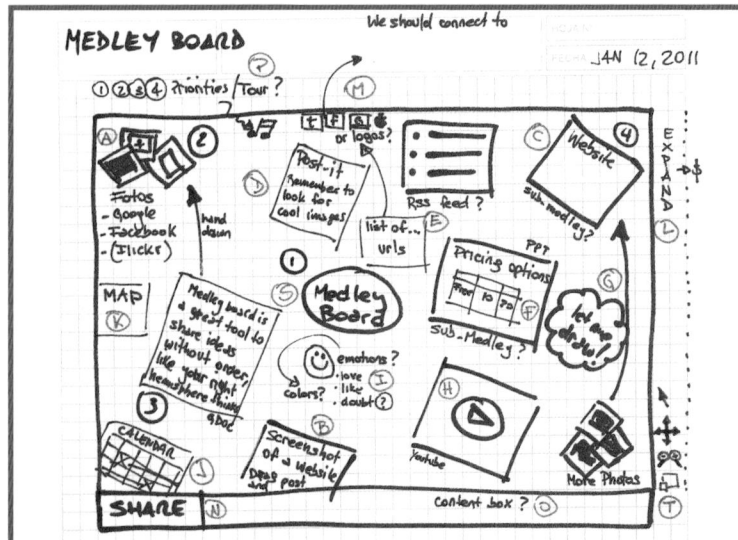

Original concept sketch for the Medley Board.

The effect was that people felt invited to iterate in a safe environment and not like they would risk disrupting a beautifully designed deck.

We already knew that tools are important and that they can shape our team interactions. What we learned from Medley Board and the explosion of innovation it created was more profound: It's really the broader environment that gives rise to connected teamwork.

And to be sure, research shows that the environment where collaboration happens is the single biggest factor influencing team success.[1]

So if you want to improve collaboration behaviors and results, focus on setting up the right environments. Collaboration spaces power connected teams.

Our notion of collaboration spaces now includes both physical and digital spaces and embraces hybrid collaboration, VR, and beyond. It's really about the entire tool set a team has to collaborate. The term "space" itself here also includes the dynamic and metaphoric spaces in which collaboration occurs, the social boundaries of shared work.

Having observed—over a decade of working with hundreds of teams—that the spaces in which we interact have a deep influence on the nature of the collaboration that happens in them, we're forced to ask a necessary question: How can we organize the tools and environments of collaboration to foster exceptional teamwork?

---

1   See in particular the work of Richard Hackman, e.g., *Leading Teams* (2002) and Martine Haas and Mark Mortensen, "The Secrets of Great Teamwork," *Harvard Business Review* (Jun 2016).

The Spaces We Make for Collaboration

In the past, a single, monolithic collaboration tool loomed over the teamwork landscape: the office building. Some leaders relied upon the fact that their teams shared a physical space almost to the exclusion of other means of collaboration.

Except any knowledge worker will tell you that putting people in proximity to each other doesn't guarantee collaboration. And as new spaces have given rise to new collaboration opportunities, innovative organizations must embrace these changes to the modalities of work. .

Authentic collaboration spaces, whether physical, digital, or both, offer teams a place designed to support teamwork. That means supporting not only interaction and productivity toward a shared, common purpose but also supporting relationships. Our conception of a common space is one that's shared, radically accessible, inclusive of the entire team, and adaptable. It's also agnostic to locale, and its modality is flexible and adaptive to the needs of the people who use it.

There are several fundamental types of collaboration spaces we've identified:

Physical Spaces. For many reasons, physical collaboration space is (to date, at least) generally seen as unparalleled in its ability to create spontaneous connection. Relationships can be nurtured before meetings, during breaks, and at the end of the day. Body language and tone of voice add a richness to communication that people crave. Fact is, interacting in physical spaces feels comfortable and normal for us as humans. But more and more, we're seeing physical spaces powered with digital technology. Touchscreens, monitors, and kiosks allow teams to collaborate online even if they are interacting together in a physical space. The benefit is a better ability to transition to other types of spaces and other modes of collaboration.

Online Spaces. Because teams are less often in the same building, digital collaboration online has become the new norm. Here, our interaction with others is mediated completely through software. In this sense, the space that is created really amounts to a collection of tools.

Hybrid Spaces. Common spaces are not an either-or proposition. They are commonly combined in hybrid spaces, where some interact online while others are concurrently together in a physical space. While hybrid collaboration has become the dominant mode of working together post-pandemic, it's not new. In fact, around 60% of the teams we've polled worked in mixed spaces most of the time.

We've run several experiments in collaboration directly comparing different spaces and the effect they have on how teams work together. You can try it yourself: Have groups simultaneously participate in the same meeting or workshop from different settings, that is, one team in-person, one remote only, and another hybrid. Give them the same challenge and observe how the team interacts and what they produce.

In many cases, we've found a common pattern emerges: The type and amount of content contributed during a given session varies across groups. Teams together in a physical space tend to take more time discussing the topic at hand and therefore generally produce a lower volume of content (e.g., ideas during brainstorming) than online-only participants, who have fewer conversations but outpace the volume of content generated greatly. Hybrid teams theoretically can have the best of both worlds, but often get more distracted with an imbalance of interaction that they can end up being less productive than other group types.

Regardless of your starting point, someone always has to pay attention to the pace and rhythm of the collaboration and how methods are used to guide the interaction. Collaboration design considers space, but extends beyond it to shape the overall experience.

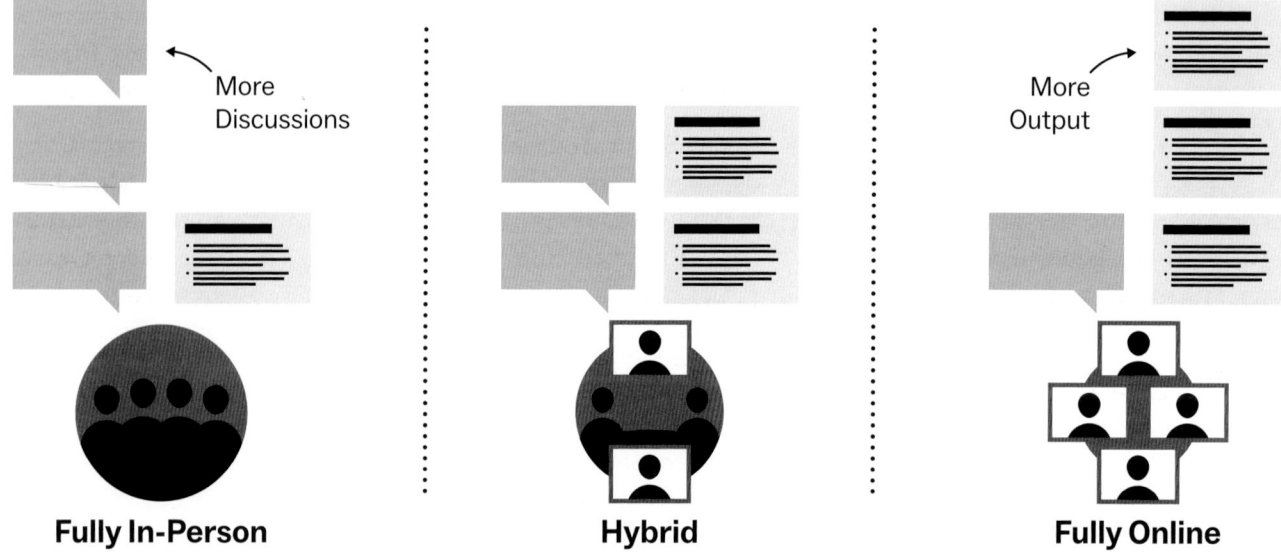

More Discussions

More Output

Fully In-Person   **Hybrid**   **Fully Online**

Many benefits of VR have come to light in our work with the medium:

VR removes constraints. Teams can do things that weren't possible when they were limited to current spaces and tools. It's the best of both worlds: a sense of physical space and the intimacy of in-person communication along with benefits of digital technology.

VR increases connection. The immersive experience of VR gives participants a heightened sense of awareness of others. Our experience indicates that teams can connect in VR at a level on par with in-person interactions.

VR accelerates problem-solving. The design of the space can support team activities in a way that makes a strong impression in VR. Team members tend to have greater comprehension, retention, and alignment.

The upshot of these benefits is that the quality of the results we've found so far when testing with various audiences is generally better when teams collaborate in VR.

If your team is ready for it, use VR as a complementary mode of collaboration when it makes sense. As our colleague Douglas Ferguson, president of Voltage Control, a leadership consultancy specializing in facilitation and collaboration, reminds us, "A headset is cheaper than a flight."

Virtual reality spaces. You've heard the hype by now: Virtual reality is coming. But is there a real benefit to VR? Will it have a meaningful place in work settings? Most importantly, can VR enhance collaboration? We believe the answer is yes—though exactly when VR becomes a regular channel for collaboration is still to be seen. From what we've observed so far, VR can add great value to teamwork and to creating human connection. Core to the benefit of VR is the immersive experience it provides. If the medium is the message, VR packs a powerful one.

No one expects employees to wear a headset eight hours a day. Instead, the key is to recognize that VR has its time and place. It's also important to keep in mind that work done in VR isn't trapped in or limited to VR spaces. Systems currently integrate with other tools to work outside of virtual spaces.

With this in mind, a key issue to consider is the transition in and out of the VR spaces. It's not just a practical issue, but also a cognitive one. How do you guide participants into the right frame of mind? How to set new expectations when moving into VR?

Storytelling is a large part of the process. Don Carson, design director at Mighty Coconut and VR design expert, told us in a panel discussion: "VR isn't a linear type of storytelling, rather it's an environmental way in which you design and layout spaces so when people enter they have a sense of familiarity and can relate to it. One way to do that is to show that someone else was there or already living in it, or activity has happened."

We've found creating storyboards of the collaboration in VR helps tell an overall experiential story. This way you can grasp the various elements and parts of the interaction before creating a VR experience.

For instance, teams at Mural have been focusing on using VR for team building and forming deeper connections.

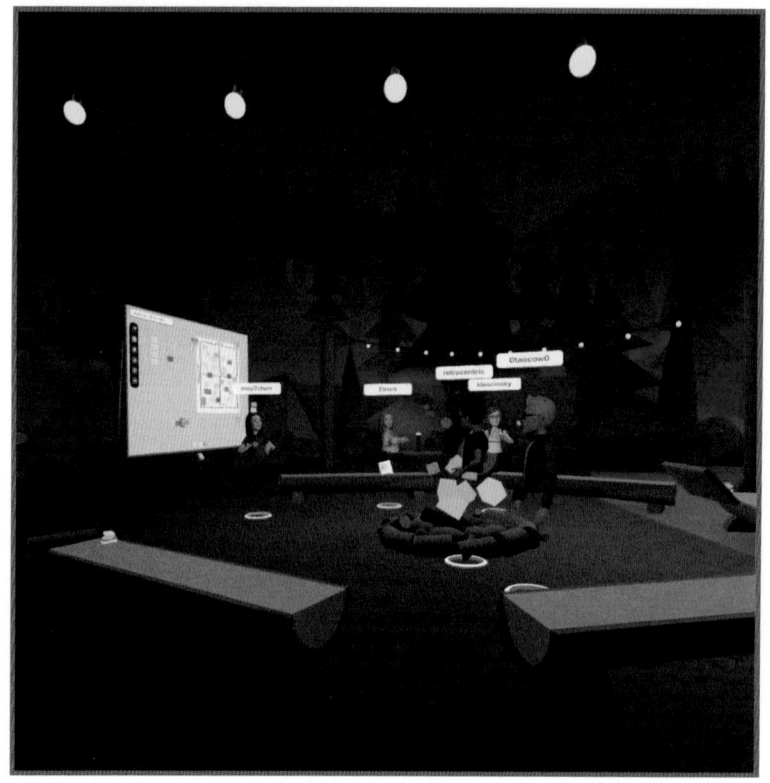

Designing Collaboration Spaces

How does a collaboration designer start intentionally designing the optimal environment teams need to thrive? Building from some initial observations, you can conceptualize updated spaces within the span of a short workshop. Here is a recipe of methods we recommend to begin your journey:

Fly-on-the-Wall Observation. Innovation begins with keen observation. This method is an unobtrusive way to get a real-world view of how teams in your organization collaborate. It's simple: Select a few teams to follow, and go out to watch them in action (e.g., during meetings and working sessions). Focus in particular on the spaces in which they work and the tools they use. Silently observe as they interact and take notes, screenshots, and photos. (This takes place over several hours across multiple days.)

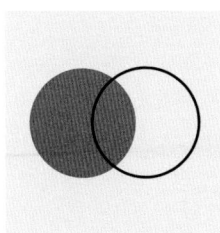

Concept Mapping. From the findings gathered during your observations, map out the various concepts you identified—people, places, tools, and so on. Illustrate the relationships between them by drawing a diagram of the objects (nouns) in your model connected with relational links (verbs). Circle and label related groupings and themes that emerge from your diagram. (1 hour)

Rose, Thorn, Bud. Reflect on your insights of your concept model so far by noting the positives (roses), negatives (thorns), and things that have potential (buds). Do this in a group to gather diverse perspectives on the collaboration spaces you're evaluating. In an additional step, you can cluster the roses, thorns, and buds by theme to see what patterns emerge before brainstorming solutions. (30 minutes)

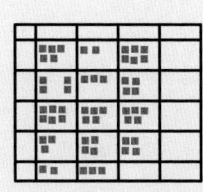

Creative Matrix. Generate many wide-ranging ideas using a large grid to guide brainstorming. Designate different types of collaborators in your organization across the top; then designate themes or topics for solution in the rows. The rows can be the jobs to be done of any collaboration space. (30 minutes)

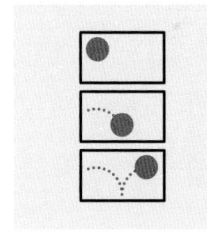

Storyboarding. Select ideas from the creative matrix to develop in a series of images to show a scenario of use. In a story, describe how improved collaboration spaces might look in your organization. (1 hour)

The Jobs of Common Spaces

From our research and observations, we've identified a core set of jobs to be done that teams need from the space they share to collaborate in. As you design collaboration spaces, keep these in mind regardless of where and how teams interact. The nature of the different tools that are used for each job puts a boundary on and defines how collaboration will happen in common space:

Share, store, and archive materials in a central location. Teams need a way to exchange information in different formats.

Make decisions together in real time. Team members need to speak directly with colleagues, both individually and in groups.

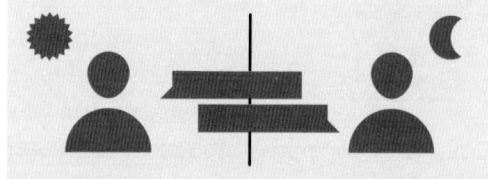

Communicate asynchronously. Keeping your team's momentum going in between touch points can be challenging, especially if you're working across time zones.

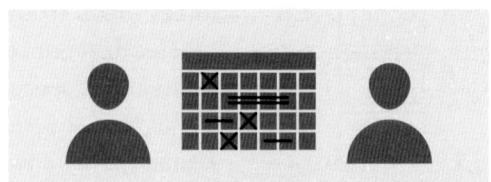

Plan, track, and manage workflows. Collaboration requires coordination. Having good planning methods keeps your team more efficient.

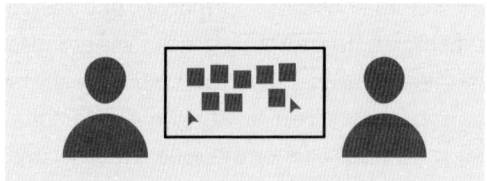

Enable creative visual problem-solving. Mapping out your team's collective thoughts is key to fostering common understanding and decision-making.

We can group these jobs to be done into four major and connected categories: dynamic communication, visual collaboration, playful spaces, and adaptive spaces.

> "Quality collaboration — the kind of efforts that have driven breakthroughs in science, the arts, and technology — occurs with neither the frequency nor the intensity it should, in part because there are few tools explicitly designed to encourage or support it." —Michael Schrage in *Shared Minds*

Enable Dynamic Communication

Collaboration spaces require a robust but flexible means of communication. Ironically, given the proliferation of digital channels for communication, modern teams often struggle to communicate effectively. Email, chat, documents, presentations, spreadsheets, and video calls each impose unique, stringent effects on communication.

For example, speech-based communication platforms naturally lead to linear thinking through structured sentences, special vocabularies, and even the individual personality traits of the speaker (e.g., whether they're introverted or extroverted). As easy as these tools often make it to communicate, they also introduce limitations, exclusivity, confusion, noise, and even distraction.

For modern teams, too often the underlying structure of communication tools dictates the collaboration—not just what's possible, but how it feels to work together. Teams need a collaboration space that supports what we call "dynamic communication." Dynamic communication means that teams have the freedom to share information and ideas however they need to be shared to increase understanding.

Spaces that support dynamic communication allow participants to interpret, react, iterate, understand, and adapt what's shared in ways that increase understanding, develop context, and support nuance. Thinking about collaboration space in a dynamic sense allows collaboration designers to not just coordinate team members, but set the conditions for exceptional teamwork to flourish.

Create visual spaces for collaboration

Can you imagine playing chess without the chess board? In a scene from the hit miniseries *The Queen's Gambit*, the leading characters engage in a game by calling out moves verbally. Very few people can actually play chess in their heads: the board helps players to offload cognitive processing of possible moves by visualizing patterns. It's a critical part of the problem-solving process.

The human brain processes visual information differently than text. We're able to understand patterns and relationships in a unique way when we see concepts visualized. But the brain also ties vision and language together. Since we can talk about what we see, it makes sense that these systems must connect.

Visualizing thoughts makes them tangible. That makes it a whole lot easier for teams to share mindspace and build on each others' ideas. Visual spaces naturally lend themselves to the dynamic communication that teams need to explore ideas, understand problems, and innovate.

In this sense, visual tools are like "idea colliders." In physics, innovation is achieved by smashing particles together in particle colliders. With imagination, we need the right technology and techniques to combine and recombine ideas in unique ways.

Visualization has many impacts on team collaboration:

Visualization makes it real. If it's not documented, it didn't happen. Visualizing work together makes it tangible. Teams can then find new ways to create context, explore nuance, and make sense together.

Visualization invites participation. Diverse perspectives emerge from visual collaboration because everyone can join in. Often, people who might be reticent in meetings and workshops are suddenly the "loudest" in the visual conversation. Getting people to mobilize their thoughts empowers everyone to contribute on equal footing.

Visualization is playful. It's just fun to work with pictures, shapes, and colors. People can express themselves and their thoughts in a playful manner.

Visualization builds shared understanding. A picture is worth a thousand words, as they say, and visualization goes far to build alignment across team members. When imagination is expressed visually, perspectives are aligned and reality can be negotiated collectively.

Imagine enhancing the brain power of all the members of a large company with the added capacity to process ideas and information visually. What if teams were equipped with tools and skills to solve challenges together better visually? What if they were able to make decisions quicker by seeing solutions in front of their eyes? What if you scaled efficient visual collaboration from team to team across your whole organization?

Consider how Zapier, a service that allows people to connect applications to one another online, helps its teams work toward the same objectives with visual collaboration. When senior product manager Richard Enlow's teams conduct user research, they bring raw user feedback from a variety of sources into a visual canvas, making it easier to identify patterns, form groupings, and share reactions. It's this visual work that transforms the raw data into critical insights. And everything—the insights alongside quotes from the original research—is ready to share with the downstream stakeholders on the marketing and product teams.

Design space to play

Not only is our visual perception fast, visual collaboration can also happen quickly. It's easy to visualize a conversation on the fly and record a conversation graphically as it happens verbally.

Richard also leverages user-journey mapping and service blueprinting to determine opportunities for improving customer experience and planning new features. By visualizing data in these frameworks, his whole team is able to determine gaps in the product or experience that need to be tackled.

Working visually is key to getting alignment. As Richard told us, "We can ensure that the decisions that we're making are the right decisions, both for our company and for our user."

In his book *Serious Play* (2000), Michael Schrage contends that "the key to successful collaboration is the creation and management of 'shared space.'" But conversations and analysis are not enough for innovation. It's ultimately about play.

Play helps teams collaborate better by sparking curiosity and wonderment. Giving your teams space—and permission—to play is a critical step in unleashing their collective imagination. This kind of "play" doesn't just mean having fun in a frivolous way. No, as Schrage shows, play is serious business.

Beyond making work fun and engaging, having space for serious play delivers real results. Numerous studies show improved ideation and innovation when play is involved. Playing to win generates a certain drive in teams.

Deliberately guiding play in common spaces with collaboration methods builds alignment and fosters learning in a team because of "procedural

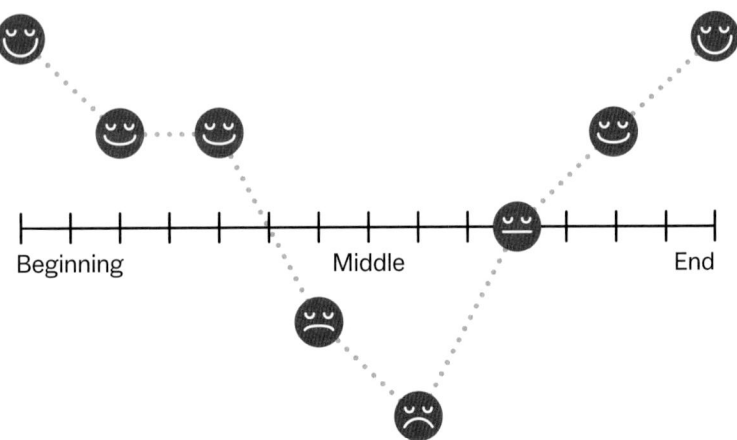

Beginning   Middle   End

Enable space to adapt

Today's companies strive to be agile and nimble. With uncertainty baked into an increasingly global, hypercompetitive marketplace, organizations have to embrace change and the ability to pivot quickly.

Michael Arena, author and leading expert in organizational network analysis, has done some of the most interesting work to find patterns of collaboration in organizations that amount to what he's called an "adaptive space,"[3] detailed at length in his book by the same title.

An adaptive space isn't a physical or virtual space, but one that exists in the networks of collaboration across an organization. It's the energy that is generated from people connecting with each other in unique ways—across silos and departments. It sits between traditionally managed

rhetoric," a concept popularized by Ian Bogost.[2] He argues that repetition of games makes people learn better than other modes of learning in a type of embodied process. Think "learning by doing"—not only at the individual level but also at the team level. A group learns and reaches goals by acting and behaving together, more so than through conversation and words alone.

Play helps disarm fear. Collaboration designers can use playful methods to build psychological safety within a team because play helps build trust and embrace change. Beyond the team level, play can help us to imagine a different way of doing business. We don't know what the world will look like in 5 or 10 years, yet organizations are expected to prepare for an uncertain future. Play is essential to moving forward.

---

2   Ian Bogost, *Persuasive Games* (2010).

3   Michael Arena, *Adaptive Space* (2018).

spaces of operations, on the one hand, and strategy, on the other. Think of adaptive space as a free trade zone in which the currency is ideas. It works when a sense of connectivity encourages and enables more creative interactions within and between teams.

Connection is the social capital that gives organizations the resiliency and agility they need—not structural or process-related factors. It's created through connections between people, ideas, and resources and learning as teams collaborate.

So when thinking broadly about the "spaces" in which we collaborate, consider more than just

physical spaces and virtual spaces enabled by software. There are also harder-to-plot, dynamic spaces that are much more social in nature. But these social spaces aren't completely invisible. They can be understood, mapped, and measured using collaboration insights (discussed further in Chapter 7).

Comprehending and utilizing those insights requires not only a knowledge of the common spaces of collaboration, but also a reframing of how we collaborate through the second basic dimension, time.

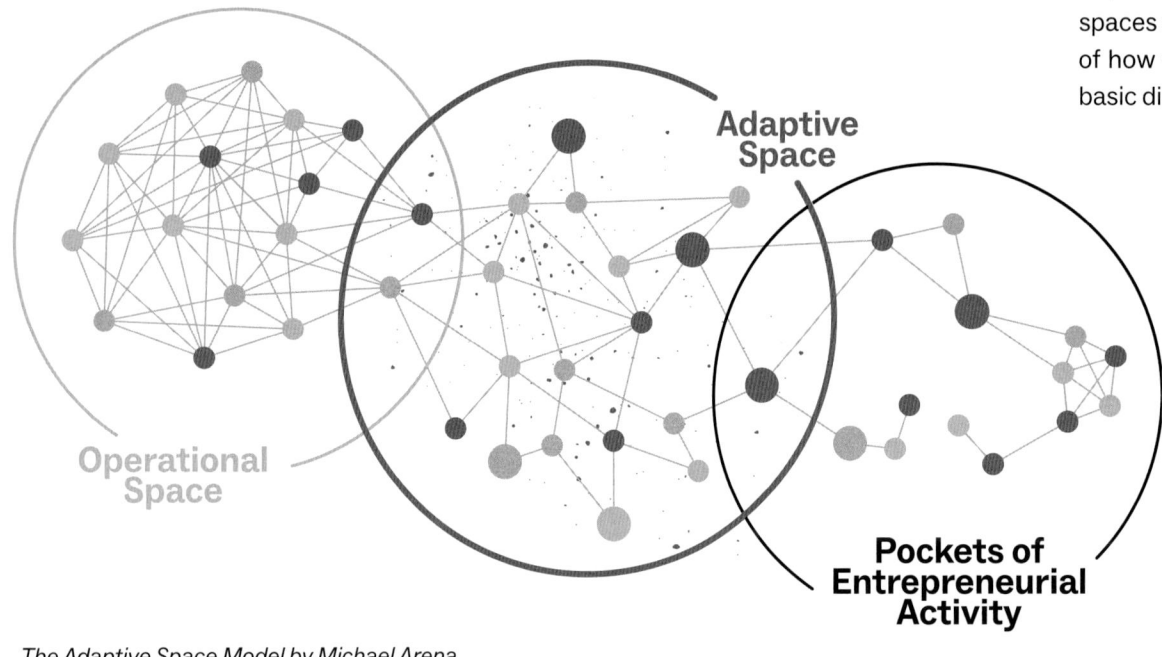

Adaptive Space

Operational Space

Pockets of Entrepreneurial Activity

The Adaptive Space Model by Michael Arena.

Recommended Reading

Michael Arena, *Adaptive Space* (2018)

This book summarizes research Arena has been conducting for years around the fundamental question of how ideas emerge and flow within an organization. Loaded with examples from the author's own experience, this book is both inspirational and practical. The key to innovating in a large organization, according to Arena, is to form connections between people and teams so that creativity can thrive.

Michael Schrage, *Serious Play* (2000)

Schrage introduced and popularized the concept of "serious play," pre-dating many modern uses of the term. Here, he focuses on prototyping as an embodied concept that encourages exploration and teamwork. Ahead of its time, *Serious Play* is as relevant and fresh today as it was over 20 years ago when it was written—perhaps even more so.

Ole Qvist-Sorensen and Loa Basstrup, *Visual Collaboration* (2020)

This playful yet practical book details a full-fledged approach from teams to create their own visual language and put it into action. The authors focus on drawing and how to represent concepts with simple hand-made shapes and figures. This book is very thorough, well organized, and highly appealing visually.

Stephen Anderson and Karl Fast, *Figure it Out* (2020)

This book by Mural's own Stephen Anderson and information architect Karl Fast deals with human understanding in general. It's third part features a few chapters on visual understanding. The authors include well-researched observations and a wealth of examples.

Sunni Brown, *The Doodle Revolution* (2014)

Focused on hand drawings, this book outlines a compelling case for visual literacy in general. Sunni debunks a lot of myths around drawing, chief among them the belief that adults can't draw. Armed with this volume, just about anyone in any field can begin to leverage that power of illustration.

Scott Doorley and Scott Witthoff, *Make Space* (2012)

Squarely focused on the design of physical spaces for collaboration, this book does a great job illustrating how important our environment is for collaboration. It also highlights the extent of detail that can go into collaboration design: Everything from the type of furniture in a room to its orientation in the space can affect team behavior, contribution, and creativity. The level of intentionality about space the authors advocate also applies to digital spaces: Leave little to chance.

Find more online at
www.collaborativeintelligence.com

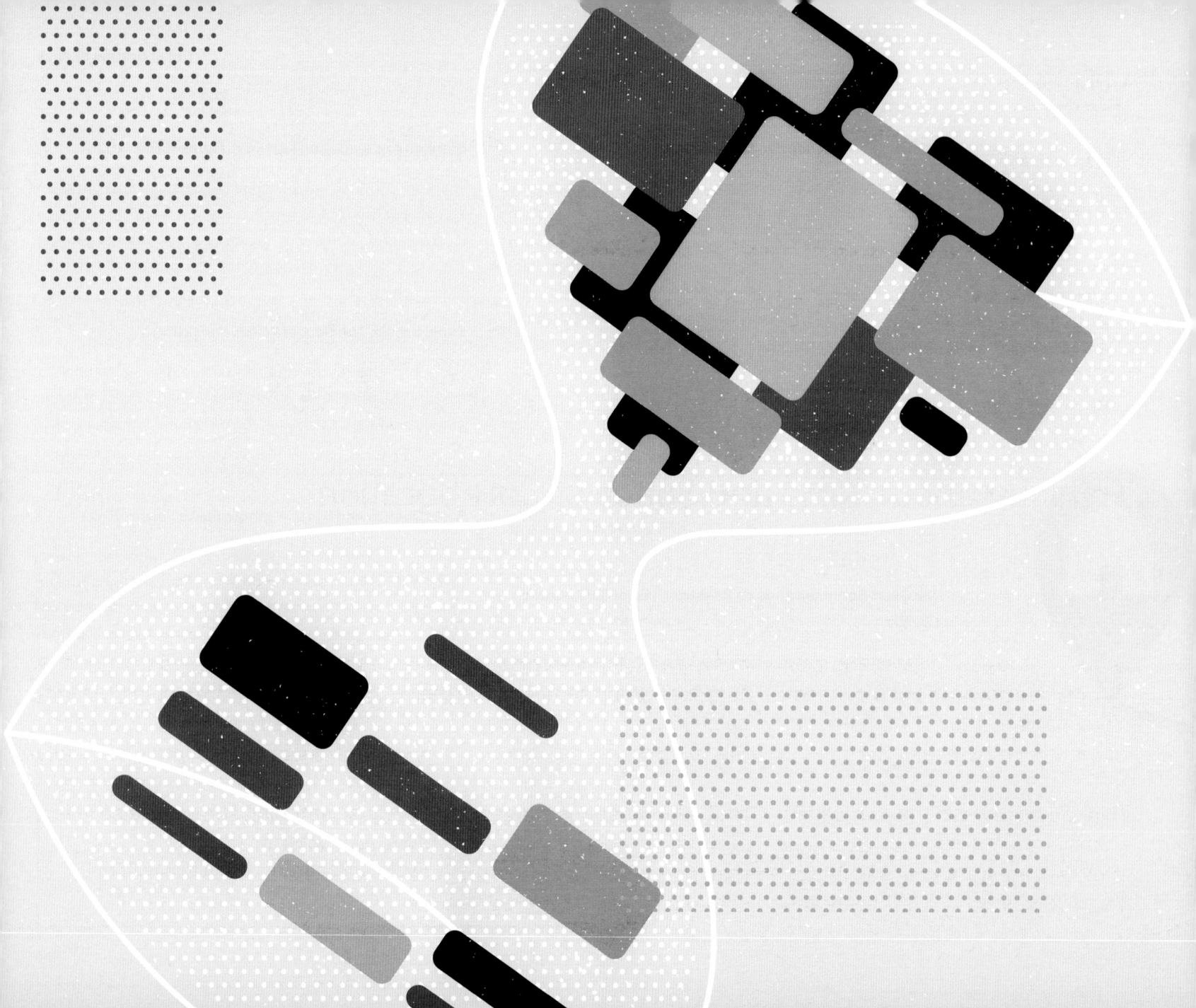

Chapter 6

Modes of Engagement

Thinking about Time and Space of Collaboration

Got ideas for a marketing campaign? Let's connect. Want a status update? Put something on my calendar.

Think about the last time you needed clarity on something—an upcoming project or a last-minute assignment. You ask your boss, but they're too busy to answer right away, so they suggest putting some time on their calendar. You think nothing of it—this happens all the time.

That's because meetings are the "default" collaboration style for many organizations. According to some estimates, the average worker attends over 5 meetings per day, each averaging 55 minutes in length. Why so many meetings? Is all of that time really necessary, especially when it's often spent with a group just watching someone else give a presentation?

To be sure, some meetings are good. But bad-meeting moments and behaviors are all too common, and the result is a poor use of people's time. One survey of senior managers found that they considered 70 % of meetings a waste of time, and 65 % said meetings keep them from completing their own work.[1]

Meeting overload is the result of several factors, including team habit, perceived (or real) urgency, and leadership expectations. In an article on the psychology of meetings, the *Harvard Business Review* names "meeting FOMO" (fear of missing out) as a powerful motivator.[2] Rightly or wrongly, visibility in meetings is considered a way to show competence and commitment. Plus, a set meeting time acts as external motivation to hit a deadline or provide a significant update—a sort of accountability device.

According to the same article, there are some additional drivers of "meeting addiction": There's the mere urgency effect, which is the desire to finish something quickly even if it's not important. Pluralistic ignorance is when you believe you are the only one who feels a certain way about a meeting. Then there's not remembering what happened in the previous meeting, or meeting amnesia.

The COVID-19 pandemic made the meeting problem all the more apparent. For many teams, the increase in meetings was an attempt to compensate for a lack of in-person communication. The sudden

Mere Urgency Effect

We need to figure this out ASAP!

Pluralistic Ignorance

I can't believe no one else sees how pointless this meeting is....

Meeting Amnesia

I know we talked about it, but I don't remember what we decided on.

switch to remote work meant that all time spent together suddenly had to be scheduled, from meetings to check-ins to social engagements. If you felt like you had more meetings than ever after going remote, you weren't alone.

However, more meetings does not necessarily equal more connection. And not all live interactions neatly fit into 30- or 60-minute blocks of time. During the pandemic, we learned that more meetings did not mean better results.

---

1   Leslie A. Perlow, Constance Noonan Hadley, and Eunice Eun, "Stop the Meeting Madness," *Harvard Business Review* (Jul 2017).

2   Ashley Whillans, Dave Feldman, and Damian Wisniewski, "The Psychology Behind Meeting Overload," *Harvard Business Review* (Nov 2021).

Modes of Collaboration

We'd venture to say meeting culture is broken. Really, it's been broken for a long time, and we'd like to help people understand the problem and change how they collaborate. Poorly designed meetings can be indicative of issues with your company's collaboration culture—issues that no one is paying attention to.

But there's hope. We've seen lots of teams adapt and change. For instance, product design teams at SAP SuccessFactors found that the combination of a shared workspace and mindful collaboration help them make decisions twice as fast while reducing turnaround time for deliverables.

The way they held meetings changed, and there was something bigger at play, too. A senior vice president there told us it had to do with the way they managed—or didn't manage—time: "The power of an asynchronous-working model [with Mural] ... is underestimated."

Bringing more intention to the practice of collaboration delivered real results for SAP. Distributed teams were able to work better across time zones and increase asynchronous collaboration with a common space purpose made for it. As a result, the business benefited from an improved efficiency across the board, from sales to product design.

And they told us the overall employee experience was better as well, including new employee onboarding and increased talent retention.

We believe the overarching problem is that most people fail to distinguish different types and modes of collaboration. Good collaboration design requires better differentiation of how, when, and where teams engage. For instance, we've found that recording video messages and presentations for people to consume at their own pace dramatically cuts down on the amount of real-time meetings and also shortens the meetings scheduled.

The key is to look at all the ways in which people interact, beyond just real-time meetings. Only then can you optimize collaboration to be more effective and appropriate for different situations.

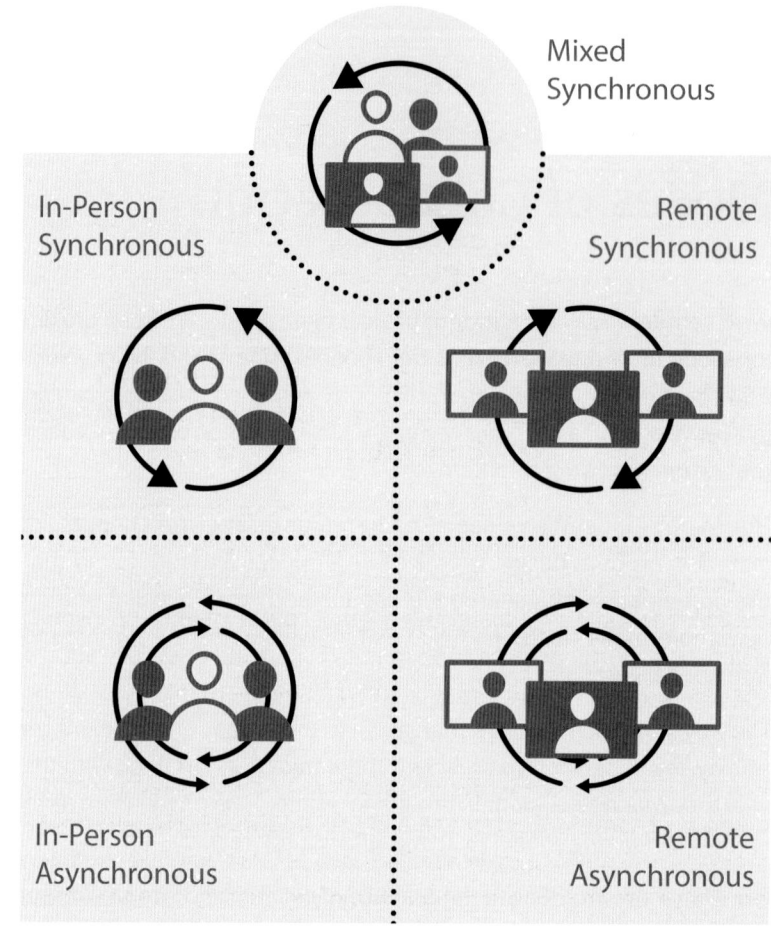

Our model for understanding different modes of collaboration takes into account two primary themes: time and location.

When we consider *time*, we look at synchronous and asynchronous collaboration.

Synchronous time is spent working live with others on the team. Here, structured activities can be planned in advance and used to direct conversations. Synchronous communication can happen live—either in-person or on a call—and also via chat and email. If there's an instant response and dialog that happens in a fluid way, we can characterize the communication as synchronous.

Asynchronous time is when teammates collaborate on shared work but do so independently at different times. There may very well be dependencies in work across the team, but participation isn't tied to a specific meeting time. Communication is often written or communicated in a recording between colleagues on different, flexible schedules.

Like the common spaces that teams work in, as described in the previous chapter, we can divide location, or where teams collaborate from, into two primary categories as well:

In-person is when a team is co-located in the same physical location.

Remote teams are separated from each other by distance.

If we take these dimensions and put them on a graph, four distinct modes of working emerge. A fifth mode—mixed synchronous—is also present as a blend of modes. This happens when part of a team is working in-person while others are remote at the same time.

Let's look at each in detail.

In-Person Synchronous

The in-person synchronous mode is characterized by face-to-face interaction in a physical location. Meetings, workshops, trainings, and one-on-one conversations happen as real-time communications between team members. It's also the most expensive mode of collaboration, and it should be seen as a luxury.

In-person synchronous interaction has long been regarded as the gold standard for collaboration. Agile practices, for instance, have historically idealized in-person synchronous collaboration. The Agile manifesto (the original source of agile philosophy and principles) even states, "The most efficient and effective method of conveying information to and within a development team is face-to-face conversation." [3]

Part of the attraction to in-person synchronous interaction is the richness of nonverbal communication. Experts generally agree that a majority of all communication is nonverbal—more than 70% by some estimates. When you're together with colleagues in the same room, you can see their gestures and the way they move their faces. You can hear and sense them take a short breath, indicating nonverbally that it's their turn to speak.

In-person synchronous also allows a social aspect of collaboration to continue beyond scheduled meeting times. Teams can connect and have natural, serendipitous interactions before and after gatherings. You walk into the meeting room together. You can see where your colleagues head off to afterward. They may strike up a spontaneous, casual side conversation. As a result, communication can seem more organic and fluid when people are in-person.

Sometimes people aren't in-person on a regular basis (i.e., working in the same office together) but they come together for a special event. Collaboration design plays a role here too. Teams should strive to take advantage of those in-person moments to maximize connection and social contact.

Media-richness theory, a framework developed by organizational scientists, holds that face-to-face interactions provide the conditions for richer communication overall.

This is especially true when:

- building rapport and getting to know colleagues,

- solving complex creative problem with no clear beginning or end,

- manipulating physical objects as a team (e.g., lab work), and

- interacting face-to-face with customers or patrons (e.g., retail, customer service).

---

3   See: "Manifesto for Agile Software Development," https://agilemanifesto.org/.

Remote Synchronous

The reality of our modern work situations doesn't always make in-person synchronous collaboration an option. In fact:

- 73% of all departments will have at least some remote workers by 2028.[4]

- 85% of managers think remote and hybrid work will be the "new normal."

- 94% of people would choose to work remotely indefinitely, even if just part-time.

It's important to keep in mind what *remote* really means. MIT professor Thomas Allen found that the physical distance between workers' offices affects the frequency and type communication between them.[5] His studies showed that at a distance of only 72 meters, or about 200 feet, people tended to communicate as if they were in different locations. Remote work includes collaboration between two buildings in an office campus or even across floors of a building.

Remote collaboration is not new. Jack Nilles coined the terms "telecommuting" and "telework" in 1973.[6] Prior to that, Doug Engelbart gave his famous "mother of all demos" of his online system showcasing remote collaboration features with a live remote team back in 1968.[7] Since then there has been a steady increase in the number of remote workers, and we've learned of best practices of remote collaboration over the years.

But the COVID-19 pandemic changed things fundamentally. Millions of workers were forced into remote working for the first time. Companies had to quickly adapt to figure out everything from hardware to connectivity to management and work policies.

4   Upwork, "Future Workforce Report" (2019).

5   See: "Allen curve," Wikipedia, https://en.wikipedia.org/wiki/Allen_curve.

6   Jack Nilles, *The Telecommunications-Transportation Tradeoff* (1973).

7   See: "Mother of all demos," Wikipedia, https://en.wikipedia.org/wiki/The_Mother_of_All_Demos.

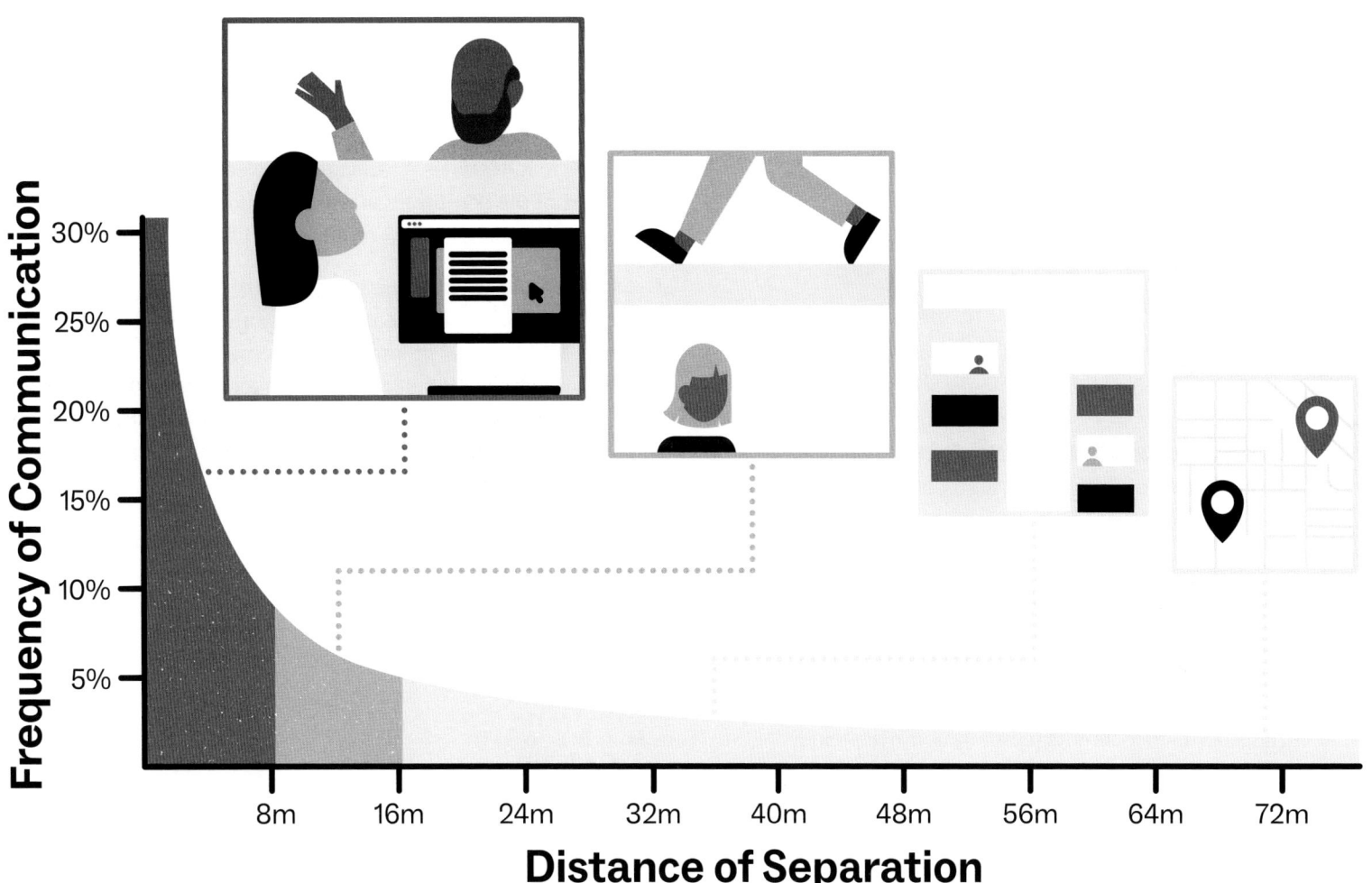

In making the shift, a common pattern of collaboration was for teams to turn interactions that would normally be in-person into a teleconference call. The phenomenon of "Zoom fatigue" emerged. People spent eight hours or more a day on back-to-back calls. Context switching became a drain on attention spans. At the same time, colleagues didn't feel any closer or connected as a team. In fact, many home workers during the pandemic suffered from loneliness.

A new orientation toward group work was needed. In 2019, I (Mariano) was giving a talk about remote workshops when someone asked, "How could you run a two-day eight-hour workshop in a remote format?" The question itself suggested that the asker had a one-to-one mapping of in-person collaboration to remote collaboration in her mind.

"Why do you need an eight-hour workshop all at once?" I asked back. I then suggested that a series of smaller sessions would be more suited for a distributed team. That had not occurred to her. I suggested flipping

the paradigm: instead of thinking about two longer days, unbundle the workshop into smaller chunks spread out over time.

It also turned out that the group wanted to come together to not only solve their tough business challenges but also to connect on a personal level. Part of the complication was that the meeting leader couldn't imagine team building in a remote context either.

Because remote synchronous lacks some of the more chance encounters and serendipitous moments of gathering in-person, we recommend "planned spontaneity," or intentional moments that allow people to connect. You can bring in some of the personal connection with warm-ups, ice breakers, and other team-building activities, even if they are more planned in nature.

Some people prefer remote synchronous over in-person synchronous. It's possible to get a wider range of perspectives represented, and when collaboration is designed well, it can be quicker and more efficient.

Alice Merlino, program manager at Atlassian, told us that, contrary to the Agile manifesto, she prefers running Agile rituals with remote teams.[8]

---

8   See: Jim Kalbach, "4 Strategies for Agile-From-Anywhere Success," Mural Blog (May 2021).

She's able to move at a faster pace by including a range of online tools into her sessions, include more voices from a broader group of distributed team members, and leverage pre-work better.

Remote synchronous collaboration is good for tasks that involve

- building personal connections over time,

- including a broad group with diverse perspectives,

- holding general discussions and problem-solving sessions,

- unblocking team members, and

- quickly clarifying ambiguous situations.

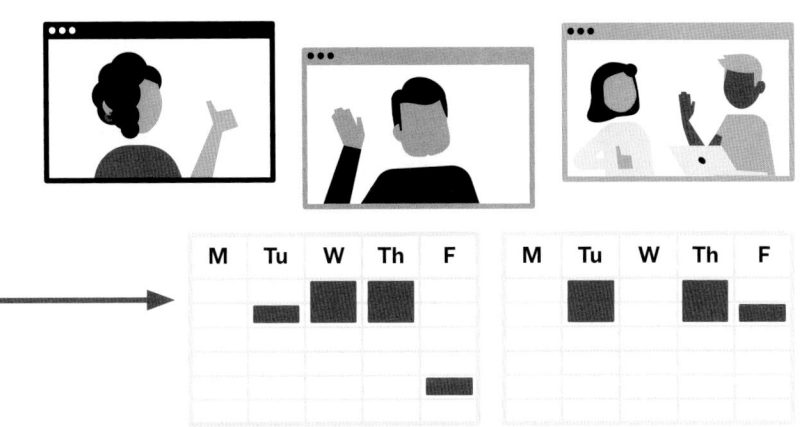

Remote Asynchronous

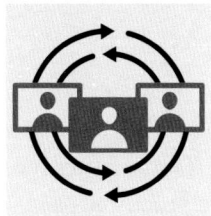

We typically think of asynchronous collaboration—or just "async" for short—happening remotely, that is, when team members are apart. With async work, everyone is at their own workstations making progress individually, but they're working on materials that contribute to the overall team effort in some way.

Async can be used to do certain kinds of work in advance of a meeting, and it can also be used to prepare team members for synchronous time. For example, a presentation can be shared in advance of a meeting to all attendees so that everyone has time to prepare questions and discussion points. Or team members can add ideas in a brainstorming session outside of a live meeting, when it makes the best use of their time.

For instance, Anique Drumright, vice president of Product at Loom, shared with us how they offload information sharing and data-presentation to videos to be viewed individually by team members before any work session.[9] Then, real-time interactions and discussions can focus on negotiation and decision-making, not on consuming content.

Remote asynchronous work is underutilized. It's good for

- doing deep work and solving tough challenges individually,

- sharing information that doesn't require discussion, and

- working across time zones.

---

9   See: Justin Owings, "How do you stay in sync with Async Work—Webinar Recap," Mural Blog (May 2021).

In-Person Asynchronous

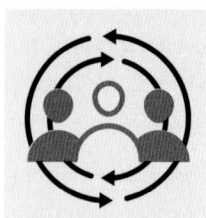

In-person asynchronous is a rarer mode of working, but it does exist. Think of a poster or worksheet hanging in an office space that people are asked to contribute to over time. All of the participants must be in the same location—but at no particular time.

We once ran an in-person async sailboat method exercise with a project team on a large poster hung in a common area. The instructions were simple: Indicate anchors (things holding the project back) and winds (things that move the project forward) below an image of a sailboat, which stands as a metaphor for the team. The asynchronous aspect was particularly important here because it allowed contributions to remain anonymous, and the results showed dissatisfaction with the direction of the project and a deep lack of alignment—much to the surprise of leadership. With this feedback in hand, we were able to correct course and get everyone back onboard.

In-person async is also excellent for collecting ongoing input in an open, visual way. With this in mind, Laïla von Alvensleben, our colleague at Mural used the modality at a multi-day team offsite. Each day, team members were asked to indicate their general mood on a large poster hung in a common area. By the end of the event, visual patterns across the team over time had emerged, and the group was able to better reflect on its overall team dynamics.

In-person asynchronous is good for

- providing visibility for shared information,

- solving simple problems together openly,

- reflecting on shared challenges, and

- collecting anonymous feedback for transparency.

Mixed Synchronous

Mixed-location synchronous collaborations are not new at all. In fact, our investigations have shown that most teams work in a mixed situation most of the time, about 60% on average, according to our yearly surveys. However, in the past, folks have been pretty poor at making mixed meetings work.

We've asked hundreds of people this simple question: "Prior to the pandemic, have you ever been in a hybrid call (with some attending in-person and some remote) where the in-person team forgot to dial-in the remote team but got started anyway?" The answer is most often a "yes." There is no greater imbalance than a complete lack of access to the collaboration.

It's imperative to design equity into mixed-collaboration settings. The challenge is that in-person groups tend to assume dominant roles in collaboration. They are "here." The remote team members are "there." This leads to unequal participation.

As a result, remote participants become second-class citizens during the interaction as the in-person group outpaces them in the conversation. This imbalance in communication can have real consequences. Remote participants tend to be noticed less, which can give leaders the perception that offsite folks are contributing less, thereby reducing the chances for promotions.

Using webcams and projecting video of participants in the room helps tremendously. It's a constant reminder to the in-person team that there are others collaborating who aren't present. We've also found turn-taking rituals to even the playing field. Rotate through all of the participants using a list of attendees to make sure everyone can be heard. Simple changes like these can make a huge difference.

Mixed meetings will continue having a place in our collaboration design strategies. They reflect a desire to have the best of both worlds: the benefits of face-to-face collaboration along with the diversity—if not always the inclusion and equity—of remote participation.

Engagement Types

A good knowledge of different types of team interaction informs better collaboration design. We've long used a simple framework of types first proposed by Steelcase. They identify three core types of collaboration:

Informative. These gatherings focus on sharing information and giving updates or status reports. Informative meetings can generally accommodate larger groups of people (50 and up), with information broadcasted out. We've found that informative collaboration is particularly well suited for asynchronous engagement. Presentations and other materials can be sent in advance of deeper conversations. Recording a short video presentation using a service like Loom, for example, makes disseminating information quick, engaging, and painless.

Evaluative. Here, sessions are about giving feedback, reviewing information and materials together, and making decisions. Groups in this type of engagement are generally smaller, usually about a few dozen or fewer people. Direct conversation is often needed to arrive at consensus and make decisions moving forward. Synchronous modes of working (both in-person and remote) tend to work better, although it is possible to do some of the work asynchronously. For instance, a survey or polling session can be done before or after a synchronous gathering.

Generative. This kind of collaboration, as the name suggests, is about creating new ideas and new content together. It works best with teams that number fewer than 20. Everyone's voice matters, and the environment should be one of equal participation. Many people still prefer in-person synchronous modes for generative meetings, but remote synchronous is just as common. Some aspects of this collaboration type, such as brainstorming ideas individually, could be done asynchronously but generally aren't.

There is a fourth type of collaboration that's different from these standard engagements:

Teaming. This refers to interactions that focus on building and strengthening the relationships between team members.

Of course, many collaboration interactions mix engagement types as well as modes. You might start off with a point of connecting to build team relationships, move into a brief informative section and then start evaluating. Knowing the purpose and nature of the meeting, as well as the type of information and style of interaction, can help you determine what the best type of collaboration to engage in is.

Work Is Not a Place—It's What You Accomplish Together

In the middle of the 20th century, management thought leader Peter Drucker observed a new class of workers in modern corporations: the knowledge worker. These people weren't paid for their physical labor but for their thoughts and ideas. The modern office was born as a place to bring knowledge workers together. In this sense, the office is essentially a collaboration tool.

With the remote work possibilities available today, knowledge workers don't need to be in the same physical location. But without the office space itself guiding interaction of who is working when and where, many teams don't know how to interact. Collaboration suffers.

It's time to finally level—or even flip—the playing field. To do that, teams need to engage in flexible and fluid styles of collaboration, and they need to be able to work across all modes effectively.

Multimodal work presents some real challenges for collaboration designers, including difficulties in creating social connections and managing different rules of engagement for different sets of participants at the same time. But perhaps the biggest hurdle is mitigating the here-and-there mentality that crops up in mixed settings. That's where the possibility of flipping things comes into play. There's potential for a complete reversal of the traditional here-there mentality, changing remote to being "here" and the office to "there." Another opportunity is the widespread adoption of work-from-anywhere (WFA) policies. In

that case, everyone is a potential remote worker, so location becomes completely irrelevant. No more here, no more there—only collaboration.

Keep in mind, however, that one size won't fit all when it comes to multimodal collaboration. Different teams will have different needs. And if your workplace is more fluid, allowing employees to move from home to the office and vice versa, be ready to shift your meeting habits as required.

Effective multimodal teamwork requires much more than installing expensive tablets in every conference room or scheduling virtual team-building activities. Having a well-designed collaboration space isn't enough. It also involves rethinking interactions and the design of the collaboration experience. Without the right methods, and more importantly the right design to go with them, no amount of hardware or software will solve your challenges. Getting ready for fluid collaboration across modes is a people problem.

Two keys to becoming fluent in different modes of working are digital-first collaboration and leveraging more asynchronous interaction.

Here.

 There.

Digital–First Means Including Everyone

Successful multimodal teams adopt a digital-first mindset. Decisions made around the coffee maker, while leaving an in-office whiteboard session, or at the after-work happy hour just don't count. Your decisions are only as good as the people you include, and if your remote teammates are missing out, you're losing valuable input. That's why digital discipline is so important. Your team needs to bake "digital-first" into everything it does.

Digital-first means basing collaboration design in digital settings from the beginning. The default should be to begin with information—input, ideas, decisions, and so on—in a digital format. Any time just one person in a physical office writes something on a whiteboard or flipchart, anyone who is not there is locked out of that information.

This is about more than just technology. You also have to endeavor to change behavior and habits. Incorporating the effective use of asynchronous communication in your teams, for instance, doesn't happen overnight. We've discovered that some people are "sync dominant" in their collaboration styles: They prefer real-time meetings and tend to schedule a lot of them. Developing routines around sync dominant personalities takes conscious effort.

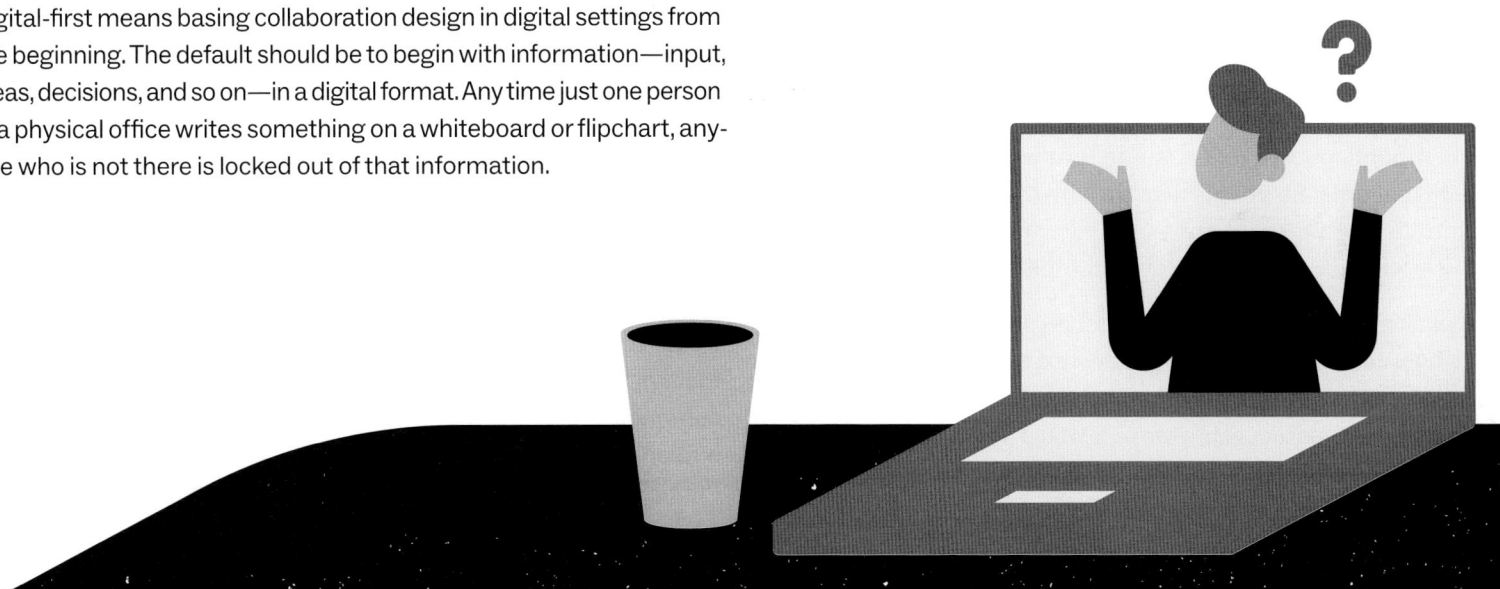

Leverage Asynchronous Collaboration

> "The ability to perform deep work is becoming increasingly rare....The few who cultivate this skill, and then make it the core of their working life, will thrive."
> —Cal Newport in *Deep Work*.[10]

In theory, assigning pre-work before meetings helps you get started before you get started. But the truth is that not everyone on the team will do it. Think about it: When was the last time everyone in a meeting you attended did the pre-work?

Sure, general procrastination and even laziness are at play here. More likely, this behavior is just accepted as normal. No one expects—much less demands—the pre-work to actually be done. Often, though, people just assume that work is supposed to be done in real time. So people just "go with the flow," moving in and out of meetings throughout their day, showing up unprepared and using the allotted time slot to complete team business.

Sleepwalking through a calendar of scheduled meetings isn't good enough for teams aiming to do great work. Instead, what if modern teams created a culture of async work? In practice, this wouldn't just mean assigning individual pre-work. It would also establish an inherent motivation and urgency for people to actually take pride in doing the work in advance. The payoff would be significantly more productive collaboration when everyone comes together to work in real time.

Async habits are challenging to build. One tactic we've found helpful is to take the first 5 to 10 minutes of a synchronous meeting to allow everyone to complete asynchronous tasks. For instance, if there's a video to watch, everyone has the chance to watch it independently while on the call together. If there's a presentation to review, everyone is allowed time to review it at the beginning of the session.

Over time, people will begin to realize that they shouldn't come to real-time meetings without having done the asynchronous preparation, and they'll begin to build the right habits. Eventually, the team may realize they don't even need to meet at all: the async collaboration is all they need to solve the problem.

Other tactics leveraging async collaboration include establishing meeting-free days and communication blackouts. You've probably seen some colleagues who simply block their calendars for longer periods of time in order to get deep work done.

If you haven't done it before, we recommend taking inventory of your meetings, rituals, and interaction types. Write out all of the ways you communicate as a group. Then, categorize them by modes of collaboration. Next, ask: What is synchronous that could be asynchronous? Perhaps that meeting really could have been an email.

---

10   Cal Newport, *Deep Work* (2016).

We've developed a tool to help you think through when to work synchronously or asynchronously. Basically, there are four aspects that you can respond to on a scale:

Simple versus complex: How difficult is it to explain? Can you provide clarity easily without a discussion?

Low-stakes versus high-stakes decisions: How important are these decisions? Who will they impact?

Few versus many people involved: Who needs to be involved? Is it a cross-functional task?

Time-sensitive: Is this urgent? Is it a bottleneck for other tasks?

If all your scores are to the left, you can probably take it async. If they're all to the right, a synchronous meeting might be the way to go. For instance, the ratings for status-update meetings and weekly stand-ups might suggest async is perhaps best.

Simple	●	Complex
Low-stakes decisions	●	High-stakes decisions
Few people involved	●	Many people involved
Not time-sensitive	●	Time-sensitive

On the other hand, the scores for a quarterly goal planning session might show it would be best done as a synchronous meeting.

There are exceptions to the rule. Team-building activities, for example, are generally fairly simple, don't involve important decisions, and aren't time sensitive. But if you aren't doing them together, it kind of defeats the purpose.

Finally, keep in mind that leveraging more async collaboration doesn't necessarily reduce the volume of work. It shifts it around, providing individuals with more control over their days and schedules. But you still need to be aware of the possibility of generating async "debt."

Try it yourself: take a few frequent meeting types for your team and see where it falls on the scale. You might be surprised at how much can be shifted to async collaboration.

What Is a Meeting, Anyway?

At its core, a meeting is a tool for collaboration and communication. And like any tool, it's best suited to certain jobs. As the old saying goes, "If all you have is a hammer, everything looks like a nail." For too many teams, meetings have been a blunt instrument, put to every kind of task. We've got to be careful, though, not to replace one hammer with another. Going beyond hybrid collaboration means recognizing that async is only one tool in the toolbox.

Laurel Farrer, founder of Distribute Consulting, sums up our approach well:

> "The real power of using diverse modes of collaboration comes when you start to think beyond how asynchronous communication can replace synchronous communication, and start to explore how various modes can be strategically combined to optimize engagement and momentum."

Something to keep in mind is that how this all shakes out in the next few years is really anybody's guess. Async might be your organization's most-used tool right now, but what models of collaboration will need to be embraced in the future?

The style of collaboration your company needs today might not be what it needs tomorrow. That's why we must train and teach teams to gain the skills needed to survive in a more dynamic work setting. As we've seen, collaboration designers must understand the possibilities of work in space, place, and time, but just as important is the reality of how your teams are collaborating. Collaboration insights allow you to analyze how teams are working together in your organization and act on what you learn.

Recommended Reading

Jason Fried and David Heinemeier Hansson, *It Doesn't Have to Be Crazy at Work* (2018)

From the founders of Basecamp and authors of *Rework* (2010), this book continues their observations on better ways of working. Better productivity, the authors argue, doesn't come from more hours. It comes from less waste and fewer distractions. Instead of "crazy" they advocate leaders to shape "calm" companies, and they show you how in this book.

Cal Newport, *Deep Work* (2016) and *A World Without Email* (2021)

These acclaimed books from Newport focus on new tools of collaboration and new ways of working, and both are centered on bringing balance and focus to work.

Doist, *The Art of Async* (2020)

This brief guide is one of the better resources available online on the topic of async. Doist is a leading async-first company and practices what it preaches. This work is based on first-hand experience and contains a wealth of practical tips and advice.

Mark Tippin and Jim Kalbach, *Facilitating Remote Workshops* (2018)

Based on years of working with dozens of remote teams, this book summarizes our best practices and advice for facilitation remote sessions. It's available for a free download from mural.co/ebook or for purchase via Amazon.com.

 Find more online at
www.collaborativeintelligence.com

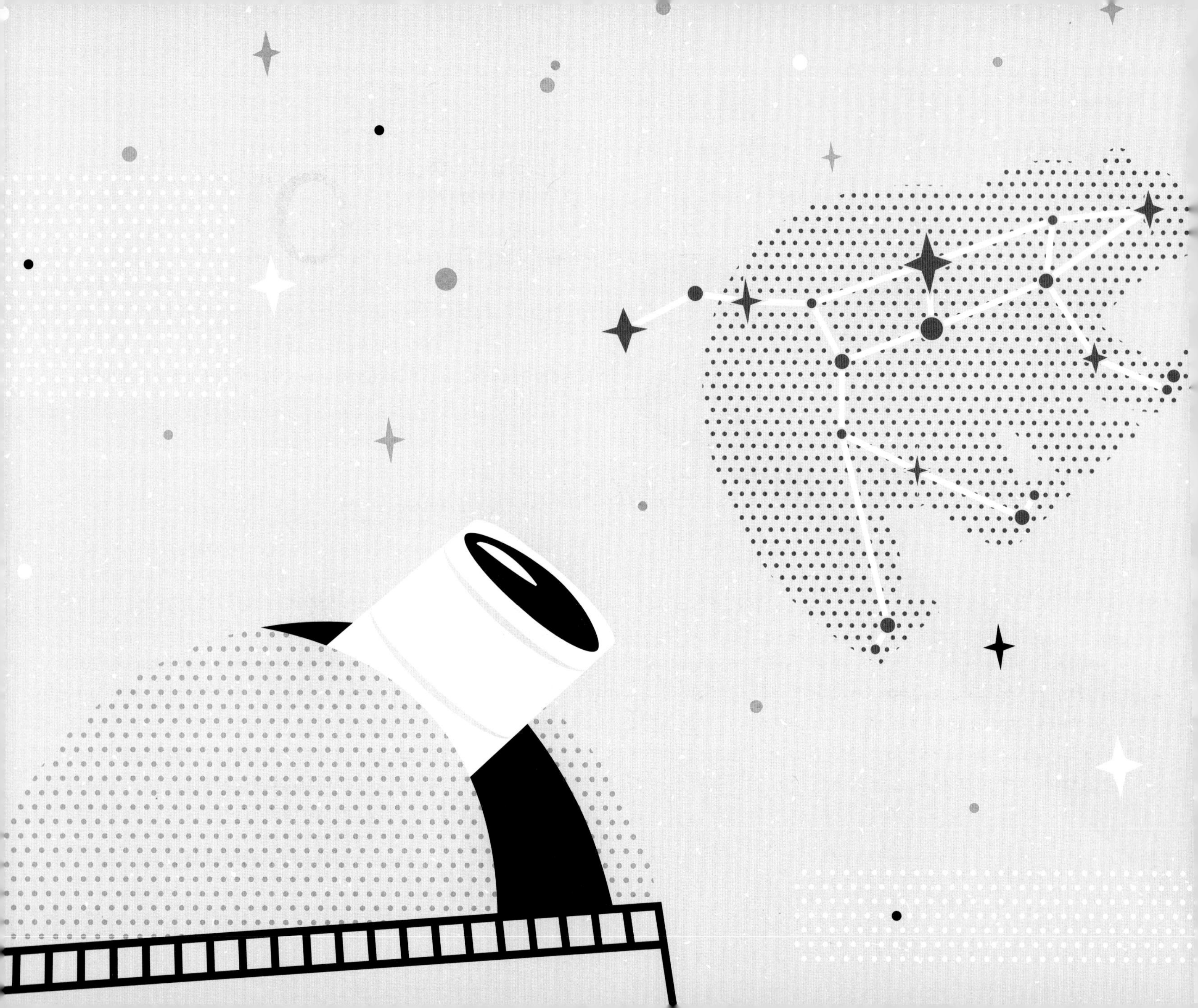

Chapter 7

Collaboration Insights

Analyzing Collaborative Capacity

Collaborative intelligence starts with being intentional about how teams work together. Collaboration design is the new discipline for crafting practices with that intentionality in a way that is accessible to everyone. You don't have to be a facilitator—or a manager—to make a difference; change starts with small steps, ritual by ritual, habit by habit.

Structured methods greatly accelerate improvements in team collaboration. They are a key ingredient in making a difference. You can use methods to not only solve problems, but also to form real, lasting connections between team members.

Teams need a shared space in order to collaborate. But while shared physical spaces are still important, collaborating in-person is no longer the default way of working. Increasingly, the ability to work across different contexts is vital. Modern workers are expected to move fluidly from in-person to remote collaboration and from synchronous to asynchronous modes of working.

Each of these elements—intentional design, structured methods, shared spaces, and fluidity across modes of working—is individually important, but it's imperative that they be taken together in a holistic approach to collaboration.

Bringing these key elements together is exactly what Intuit did with its Design for Delight (D4D) initiative, spearheaded in 2008 by CEO Brad Smith.[1] The D4D is a set of collaboration techniques specifically created to deliver a better customer experience across the company.

The program also created a team of certified practitioners known as Innovation Catalysts. This group of collaboration designers helped teams around the organization apply the D4D approach for working better together. They brought the right methods into collaboration spaces throughout the company to effect change.

Today, D4D is an integral part of Intuit's work culture. And as a result, Intuit is recognized as one of the most design-centric organizations in the world.

But even if you have all of these pieces in place—collaboration design practices, an agreed-upon set of methods, the willingness to change—how do you know you're making progress? How do you know teams are actually collaborating better? How can you get a sense of how the entire organization is working together or not?

Enter collaboration insights—all of the various ways you can measure collaboration effectiveness. Measuring collaboration closes the loop and moves you from intuition to knowing. Teams introduce a change, adapt to it over time, and then can measure progress and adjust.

This cycle takes time. Intuit's been on this journey, for example, for at least a decade, and it's still ongoing. Patience is needed, for sure. But if you can't evaluate collaboration, there's no way to sense when you've reached your goals.

---

1   Brad Smith, "Intuit's CEO on Building a Design-Driven Company," *Harvard Business Review* (2015), https://hbr.org/2015/01/intuits-ceo-on-building-a-design-driven-company.

A 360-Degree View of Collaboration

With insights about collaboration, it's possible to explore more holistic solutions for better teamwork. There are a couple of aspects to keep in mind.

On the one hand, there are both qualitative and quantitative insights to leverage.

Qualitative measurements. These include various assessments for understanding the nature of individuals, teams, and organizations. Qualitative assessments are often conducted in survey form, but they also include other research instruments and tools, such as interviews and observation.

Quantitative measurements. With much of workplace collaboration now happening digitally, quantitative data about its effectiveness is already created merely as a byproduct of team interaction. Organizational network analysis is a key tool in delivering quantitative insights about collaboration.

On the other hand, there are two primary levels for evaluating collaboration.

Teams. For teams of 10 members or more, it's possible to provide anonymized and aggregated collaboration insights. Teams can then better assess collaboration strengths and weaknesses and use what they've learned to continuously improve their collaboration. A natural part of team assessment is looking at individual profiles and behaviors, so team assessments typically include a view of individual collaboration as well. Individuals can also receive collaboration insights directly, which will help them better understand their own collaboration patterns and evaluate concrete actions they can take to improve.

Organizations. Anonymized and aggregated collaboration insights help leaders understand and improve collaboration within their organization. This includes insights on identifying collaboration gaps and ways to address them, finding the right team for a job, and improving the overall employee experience. But we can also think beyond the organization and look at ecosystem insights.

Insights Must Be Private and Positive

Before we proceed it's important to mention the critical importance of privacy. Team members should not feel like they are being monitored or unjustly scrutinized. Collaboration insights are only intended to enable teams to improve how they work together and to create fun, safe spaces. In particular, collaboration insights at the individual level should never be reported outside of the individuals.

But even further, a system for collaboration insights must employ all the controls necessary to avoid negative applications of these insights. It's also important to avoid creating any metrics that simplify the complexity and nuance of collaboration to a simple score that can be interpreted as "good" versus "bad."

Evaluating Teams

Collaborative intelligence puts the team at the center of attention. As a unit of analysis, a team provides a consistent, stable variable to measure.

Teams can also serve as examples when scaling out. We find it effective to inspire and motivate others by demonstrating the success of one team to others. Improve one team's collaboration practices, measure the change, and then demonstrate the positive effect to others.

There are three types of ways to evaluate and improve team collaboration: qualitative team assessments, quantitative network analysis, and real-time feedback loops.

Team Assessments

Tools for measuring individual psychological profiles—such as Myers-Briggs, Clifton StrengthsFinder, DiSC, Big 5, and similar scales—abound. Through assessments, it's possible to start to understand the personality types within a group. An identity for the team can then be determined as a "personality," which is an aggregate of the energies of the personalities in the group.

Knowing this, the team can begin to consider how it might balance strengths and weaknesses, but also how to best solve problems together and interact with each other in general.

Consider a team in which members are likely to hold their opinions tightly and find debate as the best way to resolve issues. This particular team also has a balance of personalities that prefer teamwork and those that need to feel part of the group. A collaboration designer should consider equal amounts of synchronous and asynchronous interactions to get the most out of this group.

Collaborative Intelligence

An enneagram is a popular model of the human psyche represented as a typology of interconnected personality types. The enneagram model is generally attributed to Oscar Ichazo, a Bolivian philosopher, though it potentially has roots going back to the 4th century. Ichazo found there are nine ways a person's ego becomes fixed in their psyche; these are represented by nine archetypes:

1: The Reformer. This type represents an idealistic, principled personality. They tend to be purposeful, self-controlled, and perfectionists by nature.

2: The Helper. These people are caring and generous. They tend to be people-pleasers, too.

3: The Achiever. As the name suggests, this type is success-oriented, but in a pragmatic manner. They are also adaptive and image conscious to the point of being vain.

4: The Individualist. Sensitivity and introversion characterize this type. The individualist can also be dramatic, temperamental, and self-absorbed.

5: The Investigator. This personality type is intense, perceptive, and innovative. But they might also be secretive and isolated.

6: The Loyalist. Often committed, security oriented, and engaging, this type can also be anxious and suspicious.

7: The Enthusiast. This type is characterized by fun-loving, spontaneous behavior. Enthusiasts are known for being busy and versatile but also distracted and somewhat scatterbrained.

8: The Challenger. Powerful, dominating, and self-confident, this type tends to be decisive and willful, while also being confrontational at times.

9: The Peacemaker. This personality type is easygoing, receptive, and agreeable for the most part, but also complacent.

These types are not exclusive. Any one person may have a dominant personality archetype but act like others in different situations.

Another existing framework to draw from is Dawna Markova and Angie McArthur's notion of thinking talents, found in their book *Collaborative Intelligence* (2015). These are the particular talents individuals excel at and enjoy applying to problem-solving. We all have some thinking talent.

Through extensive research, Markova and McArthur have identified 35 talents mapped into 4 separate categories: analytical, innovative, procedural, and relational. Overlaying the dominant talents of an entire team can reveal key strengths and weaknesses.

Understanding the individual profiles of team members is important, but we can also look at the behavior profile of a team as a unit. By recognizing different styles of different teams, collaboration designers can better steer conversations.

For instance, if an aggregate team profile indicates that one team is more process oriented or analytical than another, it might be more beneficial to have that team lead in early stages of innovation. Other teams stronger in planning and execution might be better to lead at later stages.

We find the work of Patrick Lencioni particularly useful for both assessing team collaboration and changing it. In his 2005 book *Overcoming the Five Dysfunctions of a Team*, Lencioni maps out a complete process for assessment and change program in several steps.

It begins with an initial survey on a series of questions that map to Lencioni's five dysfunctions: absence of trust, fear of conflict, lack of commitment, avoidance of accountability, and inattention to results. A score for each of these areas based on the survey results then tells the team where to focus. In a team workshop, these scores are shared so the group is aligned.

Next, Lencioni proposes a series of target activities to address the weaker dimensions. If trust is an issue, for example, there is an exercise for team members to form deeper connections by sharing personal histories. Each person gives some details of their background (where they grew up, how many siblings they have, what challenges they faced, etc.). Others then indicate something new they learned about others on the team.

At the end of the workshop, participants commit to changing an aspect of collaboration. Each member declares what they will work on and how they intend to address any identified dysfunctions. The key is to make the entire exercise something that people feel accountable for.

Team Network Analysis

Learning about existing patterns of collaboration can reveal actionable insights. By initiating collaboration assessments, like an enneagram test, you can identify strengths of team members and put together winning teams. But there are tools that can go far beyond finding combinations of people for teams that work best.

Rob Cross is one of the leading voices in the field of network analysis. He's identified patterns that correspond to six different types of dysfunction within teams, which can be identified with anonymized personal information. [2]

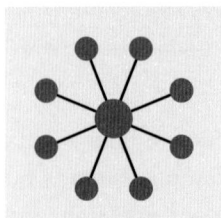

Hub-and-spoke. Decision-making is centralized, and leaders become bottlenecks to collaboration, thereby slowing creativity and innovation.

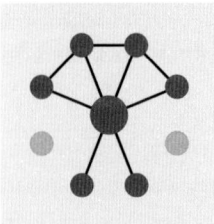

Disenfranchised team members. Some members are marginalized, reducing the diversity of perspectives and contributions. Engagement and retention may trend downward for the whole team.

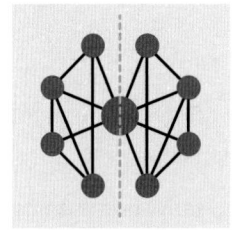

Misaligned team members. Factions form within the team, often leading to different "camps" or approaches to problem-solving and decision-making. The environment may become toxic, reducing overall team success.

Overwhelmed members. Team members can't keep up with the collaboration demands of the team, leading to inefficiencies, compromises, and burnout.

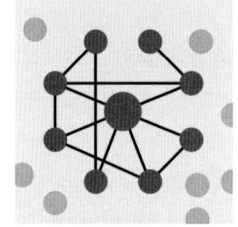

Isolated team members. A subset of members block input from others in an impermeable group within the team. Decision-making becomes uninformed and there is a general misalignment.

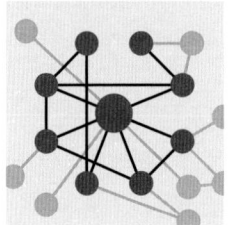

Priority overload. External demands distract team members from their focus areas. Competing priorities result in work overload that affects quality and timely delivery. This pattern eventually leads to burnout.

2   Rob Cross and Inga Carboni. "The Six Dysfunctions of Collaborative Work" (June 2020), https://www.robcross.org/wp-content/uploads/2020/06/Six-Dysfunctions-of-Collaborative-Work.pdf.

Once you know these patterns exist, you can work toward concrete solutions. To resolve issues with a hub-and-spoke dysfunction, leaders can delegate more of the work and the decision-making while increasing the amount of coaching they give. With disenfranchised- or isolated-members dysfunctions, increasing the visibility of a team's work while deliberately forming better connections and building relationships both inside and outside the group can be a productive path forward.

Collaboration Feedback

Can you imagine playing a musical instrument and not being able to hear what you're playing right away? You'd sit down with a guitar and pluck a string, but there would be a delay of several seconds before it made a sound. And some of the notes wouldn't be heard at all. This is what is currently happening to all of us as we collaborate in teams. We don't get a good sense of how things are going as we work together.

Providing feedback to teams as they collaborate can allow them to change their behavior for the better in near real time. Collaboration insights like this can not only inform effectiveness at a macro level across departments, they can also help teams improve on a team level in the moment.

Let's say you're in a meeting and you notice one person seems to be talking much less than others. We've all experienced similar situations, where the louder voices dominate the conversation and drown out folks.

Now, imagine that instead of your subjective experience, you could actually see how long everyone on a call is actually taking the mic. There are plugins for Zoom that do exactly that. Based on participation in a meeting, the app can calculate and report back how much time each person talks. Of course, in some situations there may be a natural imbalance—for instance, if someone is giving a presentation. Like any insights, these results require interpretation.

At the simplest level, there are basic insights about teamwork we can gather from collaboration feedback. First, we can see how the group interacted and engaged with each other: How many people were involved? Was it synchronous or asynchronous collaboration or a mix? What tools, documents, and formats were used?

It's also possible to look at the materials the team has created together. Who added what content and how much? How many ideas were generated with the group together? With basic computations, it's possible to aggregate data in real time. For instance, during a clustering exercise, teams could see how many items are being added to clusters.

More sophisticated types of content-based feedback is also imaginable. For instance, sentiment analysis—algorithmically detecting the tone of text passages—of content generated could show if the mood is positive or negative.

Paired with visualizations of content, insights for collaboration in the moment can have a powerful effect. Groupings of tagged content, for example, can show novel patterns that teams literally couldn't see in other forms and formats.

Finally, there are also cumulative collaboration insights to consider. For instance, after a workshop the team can provide feedback about how well methods were employed. A collaboration designer might get basic anonymized, aggregated analytics about the amount of content generated or overall team engagement throughout the session. This then directly informs the design of subsequent sessions as the collaboration designer engages in a continual effort to improve the team's collaboration over time.

This type of cumulative roll-out of teamwork also helps sharing the output of collaboration with others. More often than not, there is some reduction of decisions and conclusions a team agrees on that gets integrated into other materials or shared with other stakeholders. Having post-synthesis summaries of teamwork along with content reviews helps keep the momentum going and connect teams with each other. People can start to see whom they work more closely with, what types of work they did together, and who else was involved.

Ultimately, it's about changing behavior. Using these insights like a group Fitbit, teams can see how well they are working together in the moment. And collaboration designers can see how a group participates and responds so they can design better collaboration experiences. Groups can then respond and improve.

Make Time To Reflect

The point of assessing team dynamics is to be able to reflect and improve. This is often best done as a group. Sure, collaboration designers can use assessment insights to build the right cohorts of people for a given project, but connection really happens when the outputs are discussed together as a group.

We recommend sharing team assessment outcomes and creating sessions for the team to reflect. These can be at key points in a team's formation or as a way to learn at the end of an effort.

Getting a sense of how your team is operating doesn't have to be elaborate and sophisticated. It's not group therapy. Some of the best gains, we've found, come from regular, ongoing check-ins and touchpoints that allow a team to openly discuss how things are going.

For instance, the staff at the Rotterdam Eye Hospital[3] improved patient care and raised staff morale with the "stop light" exercise, a simple technique that takes 10 minutes a day. Staff teams gathered together and discussed two questions on a daily basis:

- What's your mood today? Team members rate their own mood as green (I'm good), orange (I'm OK, with some concerns) or red (I'm under stress).

- Is there anything the team should know to work better together? This can include things like delays in public transportation or special events happening at the facility.

Scores for patient safety rose as a direct result of these simple moments of reflection, and caregiver job satisfaction has improved from 8.0 to 9.2 on a 10-point scale.

Designing these moments into your everyday interactions goes a long way to increasing the relational intelligence of your teams because lasting, meaningful connection is something that is best fostered over time. And evidence suggests that regular reflection is the best way to foster team connection and improve performance.

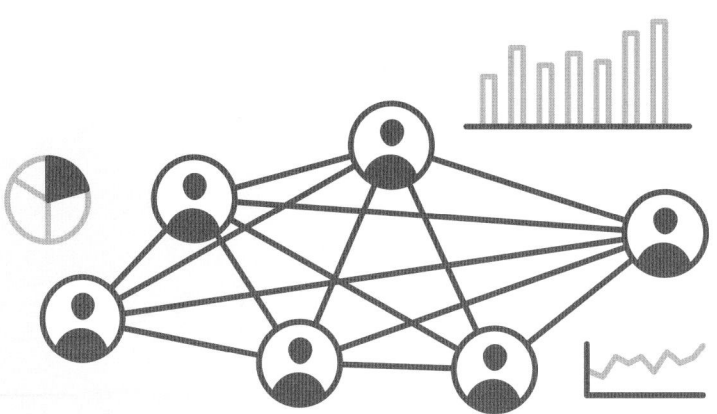

3   Roel van der Heijde & Dirk Deichmann, "How One Hospital Improved Patient Safety in 10 Minutes a Day," Harvard Business Review (2018).

Assessing Collaboration across the Organization

W. L. Gore and associates is a privately held company headquartered in Delaware that was founded in 1958. In 2019 there were just over 10,000 employees with locations around the world.

Now, if you don't know this company, you probably know its most popular product: Gore-Tex fabric. Gore-Tex is used in a variety of weather-proof outdoor gear and sportswear. The company also has a range of other products—from insulation for electric cables to materials used in heart surgery.

Gore has frequently made *Fortune* magazine's list "100 Best Companies to Work For" and is recognized as one of the most innovative companies in the world today.

An important factor in Gore's ability to consistently innovate is its unique culture of collaboration. Bill Gore[4] developed his concept of a "lattice" organization, detailed in his 1976 document "The Lattice Organization— A Philosophy of Enterprise." Core to this philosophy are small networks of interdisciplinary team members. In particular, Gore created a rule of thumb for how to organize. If an office grows to exceed 150 employees, it starts another office elsewhere.[5] When that office hits 150 employees, it starts another one. Each plant has its own building to house all staff associated with its particular product—from R&D to salespeople.

By keeping teams small, Gore is able to work in a multidisciplinary way, without chains of command or predetermined channels of communication. In fact, most employees at Gore share the same title of "Associate." Associates choose to follow "leaders" rather than have "bosses" assigned to them. The organization is very flat, and at the same time very innovative.

Gore's secret sauce for innovation is in its culture of collaboration. In particular, it's the very specific network of connections that exists and the deliberate approach to cultivating those connections that fuel innovation.

---

4   Bill Gore, "The Lattice Organization – A Philosophy of Enterprise" (1976). https://www. academia.edu/35217014/The_Lattice_Organization.

5   British evolutionary anthropologist Robin Dunbar found that groups of more than about 150 members or more tend to lose their ability to maintain social relationships. https://en.wikipedia. org/wiki/Dunbar%27s_number.

This is all to say that people in organizations collaborate in networks that don't match org charts. Understanding these natural and organic patterns can greatly inform—and improve—collaboration.

Turning raw data into higher forms of actionable intelligence helps to inform the development of a healthier collaboration culture. It offers the potential to empower teams and collaboration designers to monitor and improve the way things are working by:

- Providing growth paths for leaders and facilitators;

- Monitoring and improving teams' rhythms and ways of working;

- Tracking collaboration metrics, such as participation and relationship building; and

- Guiding and benchmarking organizational progress against industry leaders.

There's also local, immediate feedback teams can gain as they collaborate. Combined with team-collaboration profiling, collaborative intelligence yields a 360-degree view to make collaboration much more deliberate.

Identifying Organizational Collaboration Challenges

Collaboration as a field of study is complex and multifaceted. No one point of insight will give a complete picture. The principles outlined in Chapter 1 are a good starting point. Reflect on each of those to understand your organization's beliefs around collaboration.

Next, take stock of your current investment in collaboration and the resources teams have:

- Do you actively develop collaboration skills?

- Are you well equipped for all modes of collaboration (in-person, remote, hybrid, async, etc.)?

- Do you have a common set of methods and workflows to guide collaboration?

- Is collaboration openly discussed and improved in communities of practice?

- Are you able to gauge collaboration effectiveness across teams?

- Do you have broad systems and platforms to support collaboration both internally and externally?

Finally, you want to reflect on actual collaboration competencies and behaviors that exist in your organization, generally speaking. We find it helpful to look across categories of themes and topics for a holistic view. We evaluate collaboration competencies in two large areas:

Relational capabilities. Do teams trust and respect each other? Is there psychological safety to speak up and contribute? Do your teams strive to include diverse perspectives? Are people listening to and empathetic with one another? Is there a high degree of emotional intelligence in team interaction?

Strategic capabilities. Do teams in your organization know their shared purpose? Are team members aligned around a clear vision? Are roles and responsibilities defined and dependencies understood? Can teams operate effectively in different modes of collaboration? Is there alignment between decision-making and actions? Do teams have momentum and continuity in interactions with each other? Is there both strong collaboration leadership and followership?

To arrive at a strategic view of collaboration in your organization, you first have to collect insights about how people currently collaborate. Ideally, feedback will come from a variety of sources. Consider these different types of input to start assessing collaboration effectiveness in your teams:

Observations. As the famous baseball player Yogi Berra once said, "You can observe a lot by just watching." But when was the last time you just observed a team collaborating in your organization? Being a "fly on the wall" can reveal some of the most profound insights about how teams collaborate. Make an unobtrusive form of field research a regular part of your collaboration assessments. It's quite simple: Assuming the role of an objective bystander, observe how teams collaborate, both in real time and asynchronously. Simply sit in on meetings and monitor communication channels for a short period of time, making notes as you watch.

Listening Sessions. Hold group discussions about collaboration. This can be done team by team, or you can assemble a panel of people across teams. Lead a discussion with targeted prompts about collaboration experiences. Ask participants to provide specific details. Use open-ended questions like, "Remember a time in the recent past where working with teams went wrong. What happened? Where was the trouble exactly? What should have happened in an ideal situation?" In an hour-long session, you'll likely gain awareness of issues that would not have otherwise surfaced in meetings with just a handful of people.

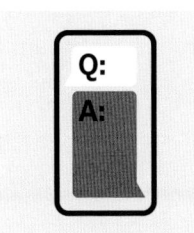

Surveys. Consider how more direct questions about collaboration and teams can be added to employee-engagement surveys. Otherwise, a separate survey on the state of collaboration will provide the best identification of the deepest issues to address. Unless your plan includes a full collaboration audit, generally only a few key questions are needed to provide a wealth of insight. Here, rather than open-ended or yes/no questions, we find scales are a good way of requesting feedback.

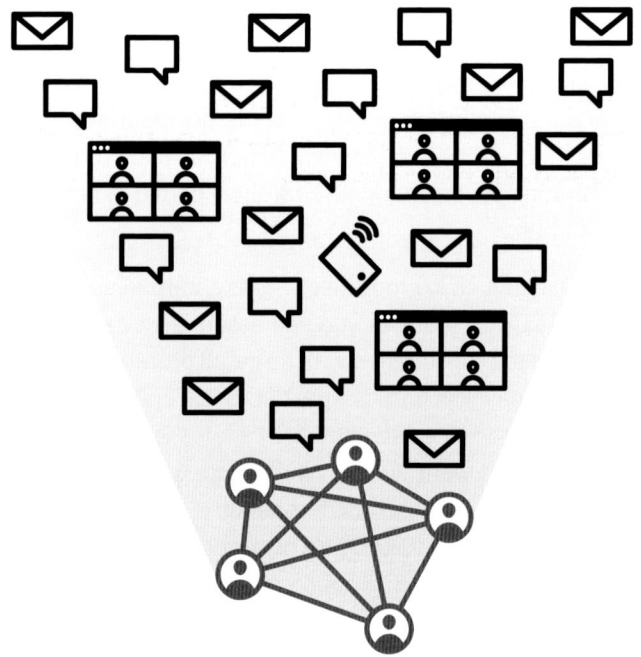

Organizational Network Analysis

By analyzing networks of collaborators, we're able to gather insights about collaboration across departments and organizations. This network analysis also includes a look at the types of activities and methods people are using for a deeper focus on teamwork. A network analysis diagram shows aggregate patterns across an organization.

With the bulk of teamwork happening in digital tools, we're able to find patterns in metrics and analytics that can be directly used to improve collaboration performance across teams. These patterns of interaction can help us identify both "hot spots" and outliers in collaborative activities.

For instance, network analysis can identify collaboration silos and help address them at the organization level. Knowing which teams are collaborating most and with which other teams, collaboration designers can craft a series of methods to close the gap. If network analysis finds that sales teams aren't collaborating with product, for instance, team-building methods could be deployed to create connections, followed by a customer-journey mapping workshop to look at concrete actions each team can take to deliver a better customer experience.

In a *Harvard Business Review* article, researchers Paul Leonardi and Noshir Contractor detail the "silo signature," their term for an indication that one group is disconnected from others.[6] They show other insights that can be drawn from collaboration data, including an "efficiency signature" that highlights which teams are most likely to complete projects on time. These teams are well connected both internally with each other and externally with others in the organization.

Even more sophisticated, an "innovation signature" can predict which teams will innovate effectively. This pattern shows teams with broad, nonoverlapping social networks that provide diverse input and ideas while being well connected but not tightly knit. Too much interaction within a team results in similar ways of thinking and less discord—something needed to spark new ideas.

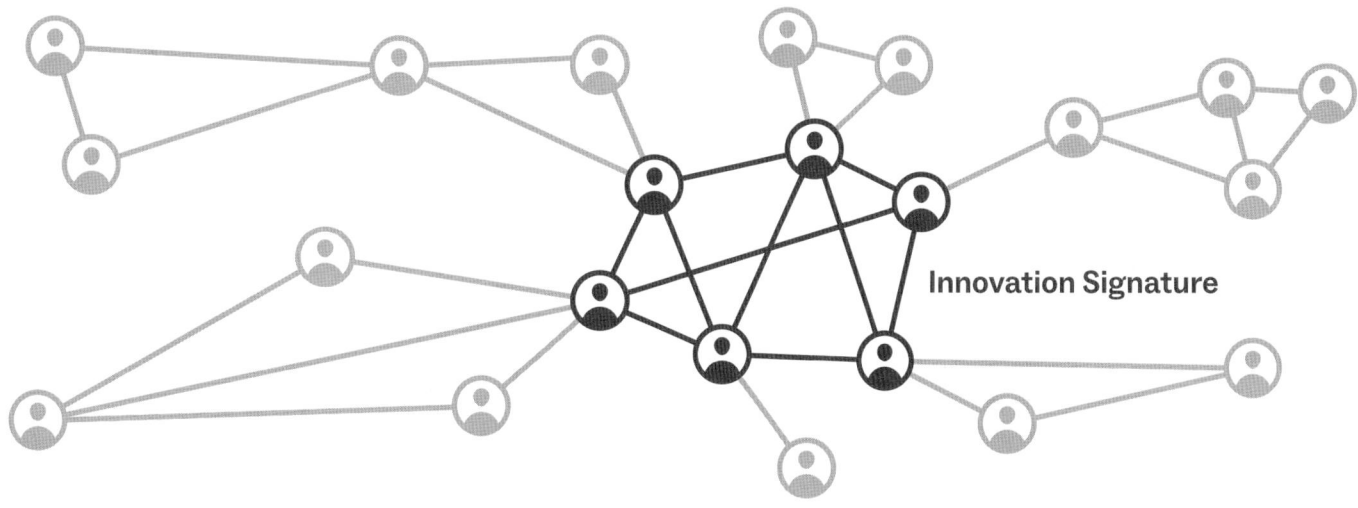

Innovation Signature

6   Paul Leonardi and Noshir Contractor, "Better People Analytics," *Harvard Business Review* (Nov 2018).

Beyond the Organization

Increasingly, collaboration with others outside of the organization is critical to success.

Ecosystem-level collaboration insights can help leaders spot macro-level trends and new behaviors in collaboration. This can lead to insights into how to collaborate better externally, how the future of work will impact collaboration, and how to shift culture.

But this kind of change management takes more than just one-off training courses or even well-intended curricula.

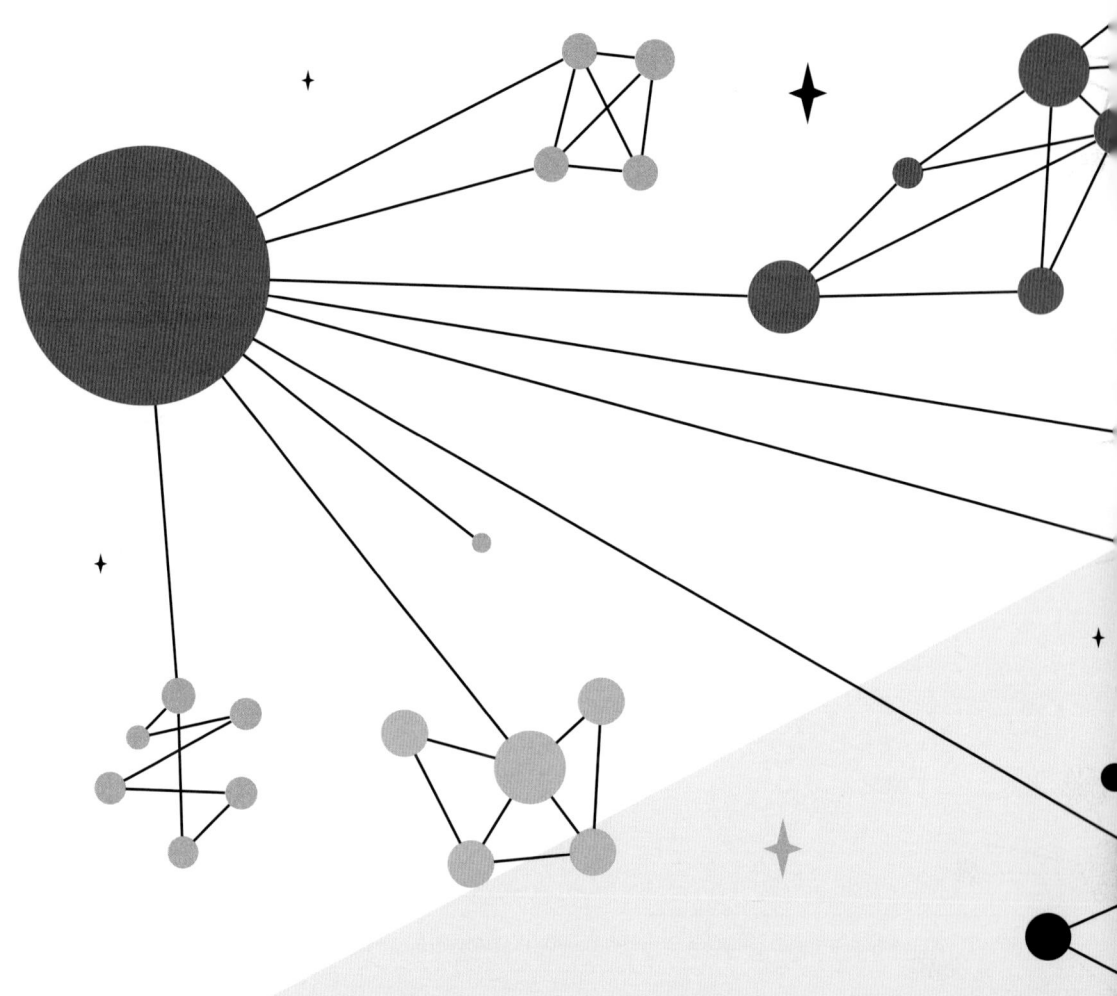

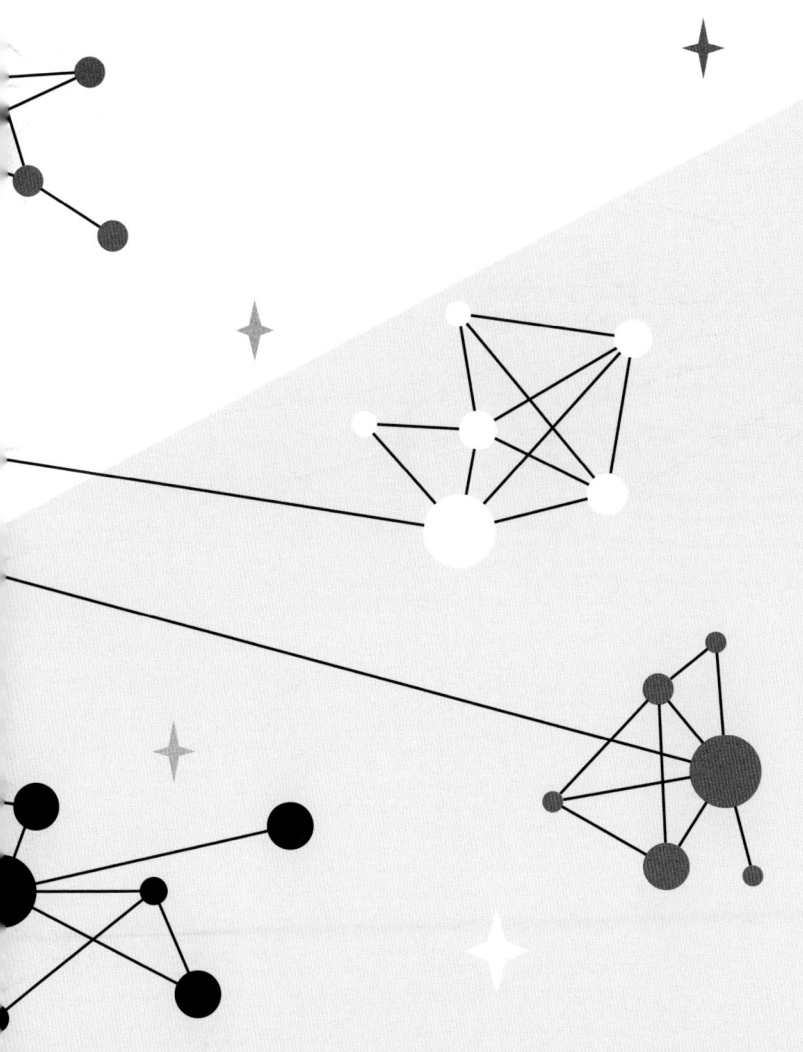

Recommended Reading

Rob Cross, *Beyond Collaboration Overload* (2021)

Based on over a decade of primary research, Cross had written a clear and compact guide to dealing with the overabundance of collaboration common in today's work environment. Successful teams use time in efficient ways by avoiding the pitfalls that tend to undermine work. Of particular interest, investment in relationships and connections is a key predictor of not only better collaboration, but also greater growth and resiliency in life.

Dawna Markova and Agie McArthur, *Collaborative Intelligence* (2015)

This detailed book on collaboration styles is a practical guide for understanding the composition of your team. Based on original research and a wealth of literature in the field, the authors present a compelling approach for assessing how teams think together. Ultimately, it's about how team members can best align their intentions with one another for truly effective collaboration.

Patrick Lencioni, *Overcoming the Five Dysfunctions of a Team: A Field Guide* (2005)

As a follow-up to his popular book The Five Dysfunctions of Teams, Lencioni put together this practical how-to guide. It includes a series of tools, exercises, and assessments to probe into the cohesion and performance of any team. Lencioni even includes a detailed guide to holding a team offsite workshop and week-by-week road map for change over time.

 Find more online at
www.collaborativeintelligence.com

Chapter 8

Collaboration Strategy

Transforming Teamwork at Scale

Autodesk is a leading provider of software solutions for architects and engineers around the world. Over a decade ago, the company began the transformation to a cloud-based software-as-a-service (SaaS) model. This massive shift impacted every part of the organization. Critically, it required teams to work together in new ways.

The user research team at Autodesk had a deep understanding of customer needs. The team was synthesizing findings and then presenting them to the rest of the product organization, but it wasn't connecting with its software architects. And the work was falling short.

The team hit a turning point when the software architects started using methods provided by LUMA to tackle their own tough challenges. Leaders at Autodesk then initiated a top-down change program with LUMA as the centerpiece. Amy Bunszel, vice president of Digital Engineering Products at Autodesk, told us: "We very intentionally decided to start a movement. We knew we had to focus on the bright spots, highlight some of our early successes and build this coalition of the willing. It has turned into a self-sustaining program now—it's pretty incredible."

To date, over 3,000 people at Autodesk are now formally trained in collaboration design using the LUMA methodology. That's over a quarter of its workforce of 12,000. Autodesk doesn't leave collaboration to chance. They're designing it. Teams at Autodesk design collaboration. These teams know which methods to use to tackle any problem, crafting collaborative experiences that predictably and repeatedly lead to impressive results.

Company-wide transformation is hard. Although movements often start from the bottom up, in our experience, habits, behavior, and culture change sticks only when there is top-down commitment as well. It turns out that demonstrating the desired collaboration behaviors at the top is a powerful way to accelerate adoption of new ways of working throughout the organization.

The transformation at Autodesk eventually involved collaboration in every part of the company, but it was driven in part by leadership. Rob Dickins, chief of staff at Autodesk, strove to change how executive teams interact with one another. At that level, it's not just about speed and efficiency but finding ways "to help leadership teams make the highest quality decisions possible," as Dickins puts it.

Now is the time to make collaboration a strategic priority in your organization and ask: Who is in charge of collaboration? Who can drive change? Exactly what are the top challenges in collaboration across the organization? How might you incentivize people for good collaboration behaviors and then scale that over time?

The ROI of Collaboration

Ultimately, if collaboration is a competitive advantage, it should be viewed and treated in a strategic manner. Essential to that is calculating its value. Fortunately, once you can measure collaboration, you can also approximate the return on investing in collaboration. Consider some of the findings we've uncovered from working with IBM to help scale its Enterprise Design Thinking (EDT) program. The impacts were measurable according to reports by Forrester:

- Teams cut time in various phases of work, increasing alignment by 75%.

- Cross-functional collaboration streamlined processes, saving $9.2 million.[1]

- IBM's Design Thinking practice helped teams fix bugs, cutting defects in half.[2]

- Agile development teams saw improved efficiency valued at a total of $3.8 million.

Of course, every organization is different, so any ROI calculation done for one company may play out differently in another. The key is to find the leading indicators that matter most to you and measure them. The very act of beginning to measure the ROI of collaboration brings attention to this process. Over time, ROI measurements will improve as the practice of measuring collaboration improves. The key is to start somewhere.

1   Forrester, "The Total Economic Impact™ Of MURAL" (Feb 2018).

2   Forrester, "The Total Economic Impact™ Of IBM's Design Thinking Practice" (Feb 2018).

You can view the ROI of collaboration on different levels. First, you have to understand what business results will be impacted. There are four categories of top-level outcomes that are most relevant. Within each of those categories, there are business impacts that can be measured through concrete metrics and evidence:

 **Increased revenue.** Improved win rates, reduced client churn, additional incremental recurring revenue, and greater topline revenue are all outcomes from better collaboration that impact the bottom line.

 **Increased velocity.** In today's fast-paced business world, speed is everything. Better collaboration impacts things like time to market, deal velocity, and the ability to pivot quickly, as well as improved productivity and quality.

 **Decreased costs.** Many calculations of the ROI of collaboration focus on cost savings, such as reduced overhead, reduced travel costs and time, and savings on human resources.

 **Improved experiences.** On the one hand, you can look at the direct impact of better collaboration on the employee experience, as measured by employee engagement scores, new hire costs, and employee retention (employee experience). On the other hand, better collaboration also affects the customer experiences through higher net promoter scores and satisfaction.

At the core of these benefits is improvement to team collaboration. Our investigations over the years show six primary variables that teams are looking to improve:

- **Engagement:** Keeping team members involved in the collaboration and participating.

- **Alignment:** The ability for the group to find agreement and cohesiveness around a shared direction.

- **Transparency:** Visibility into work across the group.

- **Agility:** Being flexible, nimble, and able to pivot with changes as they happen.

- **Inclusion:** The ability to involve a wide range of stakeholders and consider different perspectives and opinions.

- **Confidence:** A safe environment where people are free to speak up and be creative without fear.

With the team at the center, these considerations for understanding the ROI of collaboration form concentric rings of causality, and the benefits emanate outward. Note that there are degrees of separation between changes at the team level and top-level business outcomes, but the relationships are there, nonetheless.

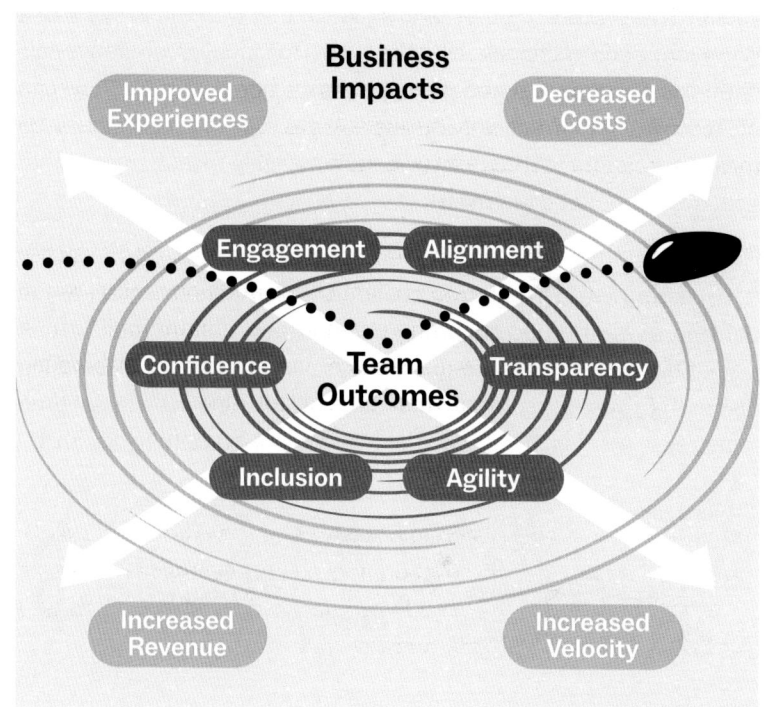

Finding the ROI of collaboration in your organization or parts of it, then, becomes a customized journey through these factors—more "choose your own adventure" than a single equation that works in all situations. We recommend anchoring ROI calculations to top-level company goals. If there is a company mandate to reduce carbon emissions, how can better collaboration specifically help achieve that? If a business needs to find operational efficiencies, how is it possible to ladder up to that goal from enhanced teamwork?

Here's a hypothetical example to demonstrate cost savings: Let's say a leadership team introduces collaboration improvements—async behaviors—that reduce their meeting time by 33%. Across several leadership teams, this can add up to real savings, particularly assuming higher than average salaries. To understand the return on faster time to decision-making, the calculations might look something like this:

$$\left(\frac{\text{Average Meeting Time}}{3}\right) * \left(\begin{array}{c}\#\ \text{of} \\ \text{Meetings} \\ \text{\scriptsize(per day, week, month, year)}\end{array}\right) * \left(\begin{array}{c}\# \\ \text{of} \\ \text{People}\end{array}\right) * \left(\begin{array}{c}\$ \\ \text{Average} \\ \text{Hourly} \\ \text{Salary}\end{array}\right) = \$$$

The key variables to consider when projecting the ROI of collaboration on revenue increases include things like average customer deal size, number of deals per year, conversation rate, and total number of customers.

How about improving revenue outcomes? Let's say that if your pre-sales teams guide customer discovery conversation better using guided methods and a shared space, they can reduce re-work. If 50 pre-sales teams can cut the time in sales cycles per customer by even just one hour, that's thousands of hours of efficiency over a year and huge overall savings.

This is exactly what we saw at SAP. By using guided methods in a shared space during discovery calls, SAP not only improved the quality of information and engaged customers in new ways, it also improved efficiency. A Forrester study of SAP's improvements to pre-sales discover calls showed improved efficiency of 9.6%. Over three years in a hybrid work environment, this will provide almost $7.8 million in value to SAP.[3] And, as a result, time to close deals shrunk and win rates increased.

Typically, you'll also find more subjective benefits, including a better and more differentiated buying experience. As Andrew Marti, a pre-sales lead at SAP, told us: "It brings the customer into the discussion and engages them better."

We've seen many product development and design teams increase their overall velocity from improved cross-functional collaboration. Creating teams that are more connected and more aligned increases their output rate by reducing the need for synchronous meetings and minimizing workshop preparation time and length.

---

3   Forrrester, "The Total Economic Impact of MURAL" (May 2022).

More importantly, there's also the likelihood of accelerating time to market, for instance in software development. For this ROI calculation, consider the number of releases per year, the average number of hours spent on development per product or feature, average hourly rate per team, and time saved with better collaboration. Hypothetically, if better cross-functional collaboration saves 2,000 hours per year per team, at $100 per hour, there could be savings of $200,000 or more just for that group.

And the follow-on effects of designing better collaboration to do things like reduce time to decision might be getting critical information to teams quickly and speeding up execution cycles. The improvements flow downstream all the way to the customer experience. It's important to also highlight unquantifiable ROI.

There's also less need for "do-overs." A customer recently told us of their product teams stopping and starting and going back to square one in a circuitous manner. In addition to frustration and low morale of team members, project costs and timeline ballooned and extended. Real time and money were lost due to misalignment, inefficient decision-making, and overall poor collaboration.

Even small wins, like reducing the time it takes to summarize and synthesize team workshop outcomes, can add to team velocity. One design team we worked with, for example, was able to reduce workshop synthesis time by 75% across a team of 40 designers by increasing the amount of async collaboration and working digital-first.

Subjective benefits include higher levels of trust, something vital for teams to innovate. If there is no trust, there is less participation. People will tend to hold back important ideas and observations, preventing the team from designing the best solutions.

We can even imagine showing the ROI of improved relational intelligence and better connected teams. Focusing on reduced employee attrition, you could calculate an ROI of decreased recruiting and onboarding, as well as time spent re-forming teams.

Ways of Driving Change across an Organization

Change management requires sustained commitment from leadership and robust programs that are open and inclusive. Organizational change also requires patience—a lot of it. Broadscale transformation of collaboration can take years or even a decade.

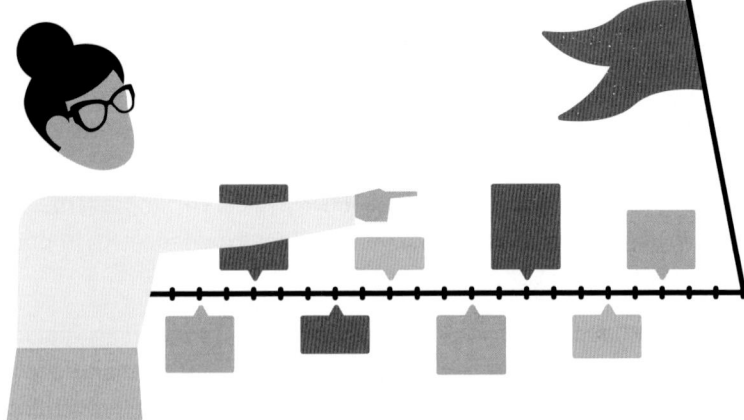

Existing models of change can help with collaboration. IBM, for example, used design thinking to drive change across their entire organization. Team by team, ritual by ritual, they were able to effect the transformation to a more customer-centric approach.

They framed their path using Kotter's theory of change, a well-established change-management approach. IBM's interpretation of the model has eight steps:

1. **Create a sense of urgency.** Help others see the need for change through aspirational goals.

2. **Build a guiding coalition.** Form a team of leaders who have a common mission.

3. **Form a strategic vision and initiatives.** Paint a picture of how the future will be different.

4. **Enlist a volunteer community.** For large-scale change to happen, a critical mass of people is needed.

5. **Remove barriers.** Eliminating inefficient processes and hierarchies provides the freedom necessary to work across silos.

6. **Generate short-term wins.** Wins must be recognized and communicated early and often to energize volunteers.

7. **Sustain acceleration.** Press harder after the first successes and be relentless with persisting to change.

8. **Institute change.** Articulate the connections between the new behaviors and organizational success.

Of course, in reality, change didn't unfold in such a linear or predictable fashion, but the Kotter framework provided an overview to driving and tracking change throughout the organization. Through iteration and experimentation, IBM was able to leverage classic change-management theories to guide organizational transformation.

Applying design thinking methods to fill the gaps in these models got them to a more holistic, customer-centric approach.

Jeanne Liedtka, professor at Darden School of Business and pioneering thinker in organizational design, connects the way design thinking works in organizational transformation to culture this way: "Design thinking is a social technology to affect change….It's a holistic approach with a unique ability to create trust within teams and between teams, allowing them to have better conversations and innovate together."[4]

Liedtka has identified the key stages in collaborative design thinking and the effects each has on the social dynamics. Her research maps stages in practicing design thinking (the "doing") to the experiences people have and then to the team transformations that take place (the "becoming").

4   Jeanne Liedtka, Karen Hold, & Jessica Eldridge, *Experiencing Design: The Innovator's Journey* (2021).

Train the Trainer

The LUMA Institute has affected large-scale change in a wide swath of organizations through the use of design thinking methods. LUMA's approach is best described as "train-the-trainer," a common pattern of spreading new ways of working in large companies. Train-the-trainer is straightforward to understand but challenging to implement. First, LUMA identifies different role types, each with different levels of subject matter expertise, from instructors to collaborators.

Then, LUMA's program to equip people with the skills to be collaborative problem solvers is rolled out across the organization in three phases. Each phase can take months or even years, depending on the scale of the organization and the nature of the work being done.

In Phase One, the organization initiates a change program. This phase is characterized by getting fundamental skills anchored across key teams, which then serve as examples for others to follow. From these initial trainings, LUMA also identifies potential instructors. Phase Two focuses on certifying instructors, who co-teach the methods and curricula alongside LUMA professionals.

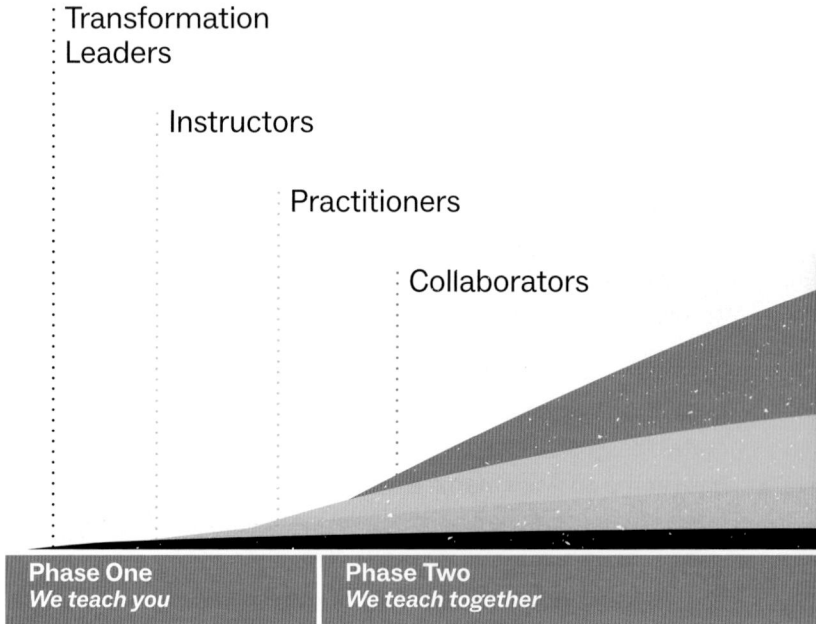

Train-the-Trainer Process

Transformation Leaders

Instructors

Practitioners

Collaborators

Phase One
We teach you

Phase Two
We teach together

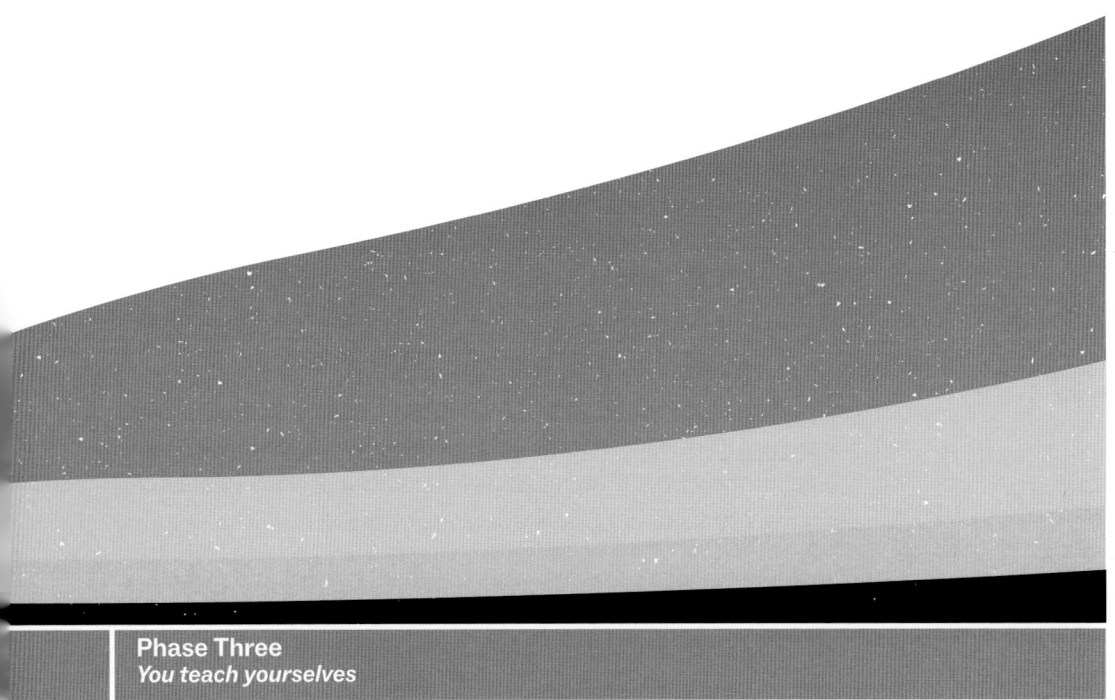

Phase Three
You teach yourselves

But it's Phase Three when a critical mass of certified instructors is reached and the system becomes self-sustaining. Momentum from in-house knowledge continues to push the transformation forward so that it reaches more and more of the organization.

Transforming collaboration is larger than changing any single tool or practice at your organization. Not everyone will be involved at once or change at the same rate. That's why LUMA's third phase is critical; it means changing culture.

Collaboration Is the Biggest Component of the Employee Experience

Employee experience (EX) is an important new field that stands at the intersection of HR, company culture, and strategy. It goes beyond smooth onboarding, proper workplace set-up, and free perks. Instead, an employee's experience is the sum of the thoughts, actions, and feelings a person has with an organization over time. It's how people live and perceive the company culture.

Striving to improve EX is important for several reasons. First, a positive experience at work is a key driver of retention. People want to spend their time and energy in environments that are healthy and positive. And, more importantly, they want to feel connected to the people they spend so much time with—perhaps one of the biggest "perks" an organization can offer.

But they also want to be aligned to a fulfilling purpose. Focus on EX helps give people meaning to work, so they are not only more likely to stay but to perform better too.

Creativity also flourishes with good workplace experiences. It's hard to imagine a dysfunctional team being innovative or generating high-quality outcomes. On the other hand, a constructive team environment can drive business outcomes in a way that no one individual can. For instance, research conducted by Jacob Morgan, thought leader and pioneer in EX, indicates that experiential organizations have more than four times the average profit and more than two times the average revenue than organizations that don't focus on EX.[5]

But perhaps most importantly, EX is directly related to the customer experience (CX). How? It turns out that the internal systems and environments affect how an organization creates the experience customers perceive. Want a better CX? Focus also on the EX.

Given how much time people work together, collaboration stands at the core of creating a healthy employee experience. If collaboration experiences are marked by overzealous egos, politics, and general negativity, that can have a devastating effect on culture. For instance, in one study, 72% of respondents said they have been involved in at least one workplace collaboration that was "absolutely horrendous."[6]

5   Jacob Morgan, *The Employee Experience Advantage* (2017).

6   As reported in: Deb Mashek, "Collaboration Is a Key Skill. So Why Aren't We Teaching It?" *MIT Sloan Management Review* (Jun 2022).

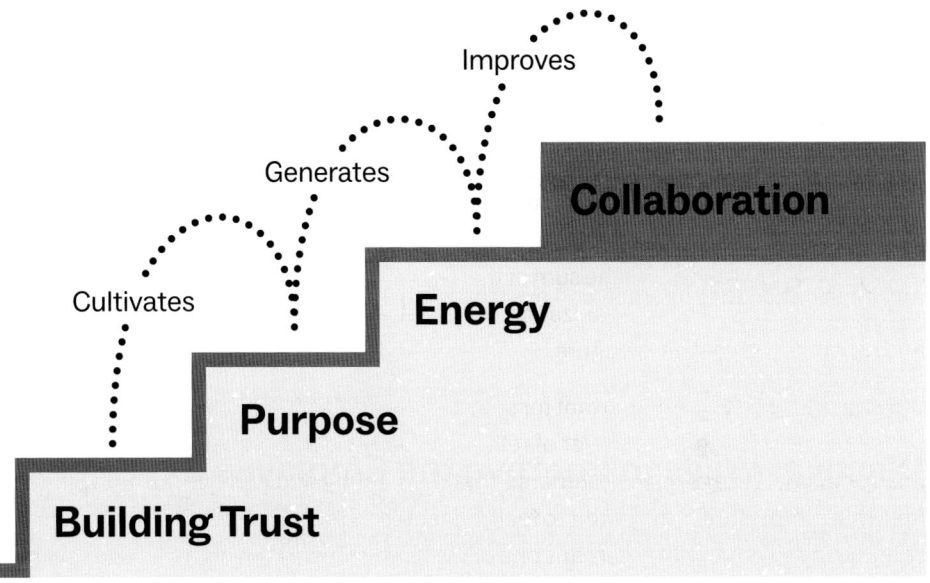

The impacts on business results were direct: operational drag, busted timelines and budgets, managerial headaches, and overloaded HR staff with complaints.

Get collaboration right, and both the employee and the customer experience benefit.

Researchers Rob Cross, Amy Edmonson, and Wendy Murphy found that type and quality of collaboration in an organization actually has the greatest impact on employee engagement.[7] Their research goes on to show that creating a culture of collaboration is a tiered process. It begins with trust and psychological safety before instilling a sense of purpose. But even that is not enough: You must also generate enthusiasm and excitement, which they call energy. Only then do you get to the next stage—a truly collaborative organization. The bottom line? If you want to improve the EX—and subsequently the CX—you have to pay attention to how teams are collaborating.

---

7   Rob Cross, Amy Edmondson, and Wendy Murphy, "A Noble Purpose Alone Won't Transform
     Your Company," *MIT Sloan Management Review* (Dec 2019).

Here's a recommended recipe of activities to help you design better employee experiences:

Map a typical employee lifecycle using Experience Diagramming. Working as a group, map the experience of the average employee, including the people, places, systems, and information they interact with over time.

Identify issues and insights. Reflect on positives, negatives, and untapped opportunities within a typical employee's experience working for the organization.

Frame major opportunities. Using statements beginning with "How might we...?", come up

with a series of big, ambitious questions based on patterns that emerged across the diagram.

From this point, the group can start to find solutions together. Brainstorm concepts that directly address the issues you identified and prioritize them.

Discover Ways to Improve the Employee Experience

Bring together a group of people to reflect upon and document the current employee experience, highlighting what is working well, moments that are less than ideal, and opportunities for future exploration and improvements.

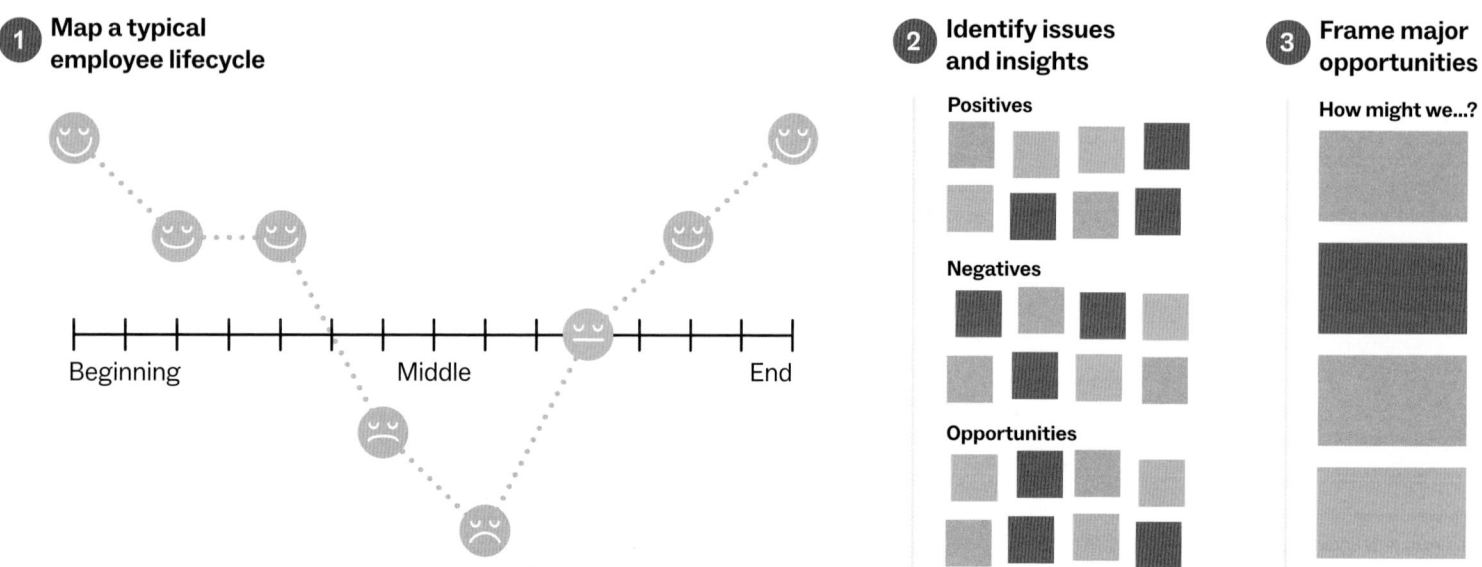

All Management Is Collaboration Management

Directly and indirectly, just about everything that managers do sets up and frames how teams collaborate. Whom they hire, how their time is managed, how meetings are scheduled, and the overall team vibe, all of these flow down from management to some degree. It stands to reason, then, that managers will drive change in collaboration in an organization.

Collaboration design is a modern skill that anyone can acquire to improve the effectiveness and efficiency of teamwork in organizations. It's fundamental to leadership. We believe these are learnable skills, not just something dispositional managers bring with them by default.

All managers, then, need skills to help them create the conditions that allow collaboration to flourish. That starts with their own relational intelligence skills—the curiosity to accept new ideas, respect of team members, and a willingness to collaborate. Managers also need the ability to make change and navigate the social dynamics of the organization.

This doesn't mean managers have to facilitate every meeting, workshop, or team session. Rather, they must at a minimum have an awareness of how teams are collaborating and how to make it better. In fact, the rhythm of collaboration comes from the top. It's leaders who reinforce asynchronous behaviors. Getting remote and hybrid teams set up with the right skills and resources is a concern of management.

Win Back Time with a Rhythm of Business

Establishing a rhythm of business—and more specifically, a rhythm of collaboration—is important for the experiences people have at work. People want flexibility and autonomy, but they also need some predictability in how they will be interacting so they can plan accordingly. A cadence of touchpoints within and across teams brings consistency to collaboration.

The aim of establishing a rhythm of business is to capture and communicate the tempo and velocity of collaboration across the organization.

A timeline can show collaboration touchpoints at different frequencies. On a yearly basis, there may be budget planning activity and a company retreat; on a quarterly basis, new short-term goals are updated; on a monthly basis, teams may have their own meetings and planning sessions; within that, product teams may work in two-week sprints and others may have weekly one-on-one sessions with the managers.

Meeting Road Map

Too much synchronous collaboration is, of course, a bad thing—it's not just about real-time meetings. People need individual time to get work done asynchronously as well. Establishing a rhythm of business can help an organization balance and optimize the amount and type of collaboration needed.

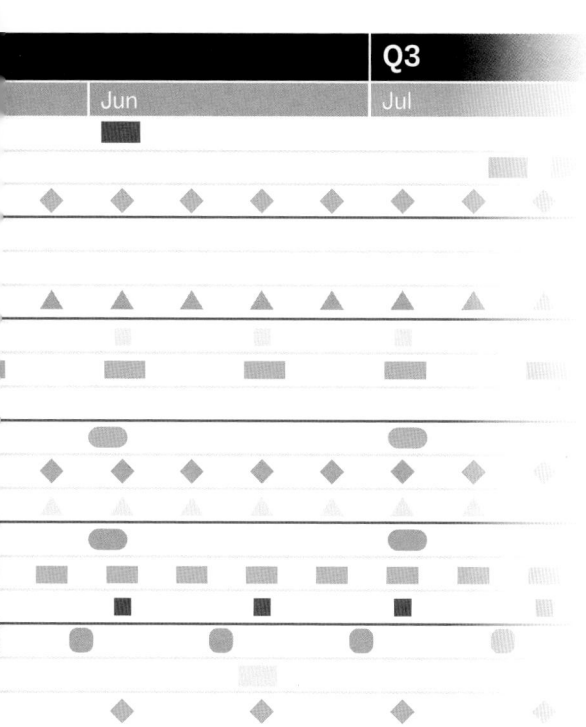

Rob Cross proposes a model of change that has six phases to address what he refers to as collaboration overload and other dysfunctions:

1. Challenge beliefs by understanding ways struggles are self-imposed.

2. Impose structure by relentlessly focusing on priorities and creating rules for interactions.

3. Alter behaviors by using most efficient communication channels and setting network norms.

4. Enable scale by mobilizing a broad network and key opinion leaders.

5. Create contexts of engagement with pull not push.

6. Prioritize renewal with networks for purpose and well-being.[8]

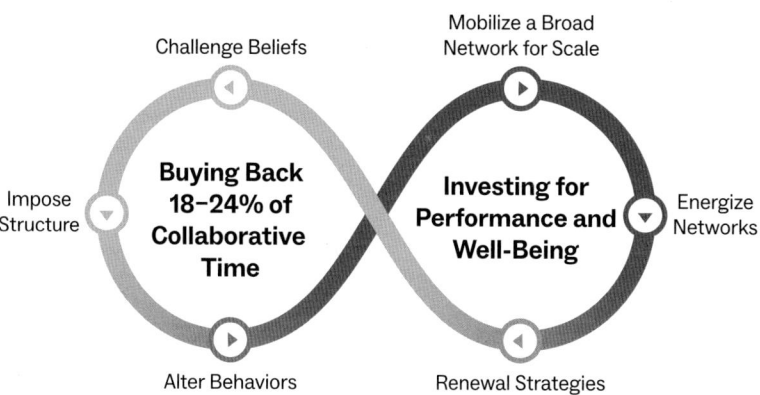

---

8   Rob Cross, *Beyond Collaboration Overload* (2021).

Collaboration Leadership

Who should be in charge of collaboration at your company? The answer to that simple question is not necessarily obvious.

As early as 2010, the *Harvard Business* Review touted the need for another C-suite executive: the CCO—chief collaboration officer.[9] Authors Morten T. Hansen and Scott Tapp showed that a chief collaboration officer would be charged with connecting people across the organization to increase innovation performance. While the role exists, it hasn't really caught on in a widespread way.

In fact, we don't believe a separate role dedicated to collaboration is absolutely necessary. Instead, anchoring collaboration at the leadership level should be the responsibility of an existing role. We've seen duties spread out between teams, from facilities to IT to subject matter experts.

Chief of staff is one role that makes sense and has been effective, in our experience, but there are others emerging in HR and elsewhere in the organization.

Anchoring collaboration at the leadership level also signals a commitment to the rest of the organization. Making change at the broader cultural level is generally enhanced with top-down support. Ultimately, leadership is about designing the circumstances for innovation to take hold. Only then can change happen.

---

9   Morten T. Hansen and Scott Tapp. "Who Should be Your Chief Collaboration Officer?" *Harvard Business Review* (Oct 2010).

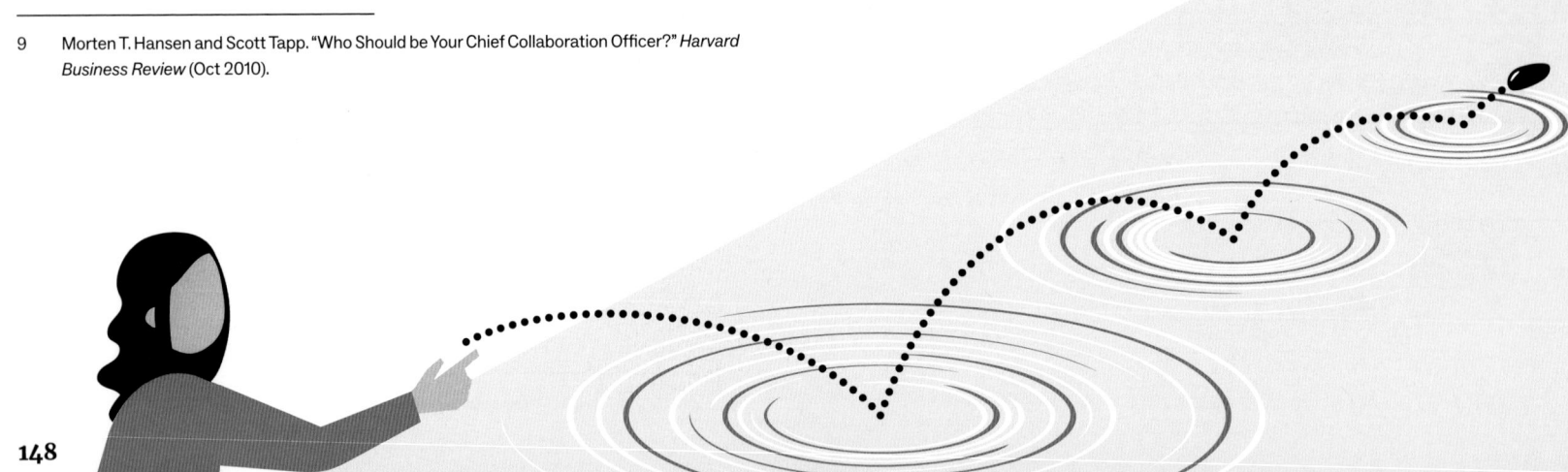

Recommended Reading

Morton Hansen, *Collaboration* (2009)

This prominent book in collaboration literature focuses on leadership and collaboration management. In particular, Hansen introduces the notion of T-shaped collaboration management—collaborating across divisions while focusing deeply on your own unit—as a way to foster better networks across the organization. The practical advice in this book is based on the author's own in-depth research, including numerous case studies and examples.

Gibb Dyer and Jeff Dyer, *Beyond Team Building* (2020)

The Dyers introduce a holistic model for effective teamwork based on the 5 Cs: context, composition, competencies, change, and collaborative leadership. Managers, as the authors note, need to not only focus on collaboration within their own teams, but also across other teams and even with external consultants and partners. Team leaders are collaboration leaders, in their view, and giving managers better collaboration skills is a first step in leveling up collaboration culture across the company.

Denise Lee Yon, *Fusion* (2018)

Lee Yon brings together decades of experience in both brand and culture in this groundbreaking book. She makes a compelling argument for fusing the two areas, demonstrating how competitive advantage is driven by a CX-EX alignment. We agree and would argue that collaboration is critical on both sides of the equation—for healthy employee experiences as well as productive customer relationships.

Jacob Morgan, *The Employee Experience Advantage* (2017)

This book is one of the better resources on employee experience. It's well organized, easy to read, and, most importantly, thoroughly researched. Morgan presents his detailed findings from years of investigation in correlating EX to bottom-line business results.

Keith Ferrazzi, Kian Gohar, and Noel Weyrich, *Competing in the New World of Work* (2022)

Based on some of the latest research on collaboration, this book is both inspirational and practical. The authors make a compelling case for embracing changes in the way work gets done as a new source of competitive advantage. Modern topics of adaptability, agility, resilience, and purpose are explored in depth for one of the most contemporary views on collaboration.

Aaron Dignan, *Brave New Work* (2019)

One of our favorites, this book stands out in a crowd of writing on "the future of work." Dignan offers a simple yet counterintuitive perspective on how to re-imagine not only the way teams work but how organizations operate. Full of real-world examples, it puts theory into practice and offers tools that any organization can use to re-invent itself.

Find more online at
www.collaborativeintelligence.com

Afterword

Imagine It All Came True

Imagine if you had the skills, methods, and space to tackle any problem. Imagine that your teams had the trust, confidence, and enthusiasm to make work feel like play. Imagine teams in your organization doing the best work of their lives consistently.

Take a moment to close your eyes to envision this future for your team.

If you are still with us, you probably already believe that there has to be a better way. Lots of great hours are wasted and potential is not reached because of bad collaboration.

We don't leave product design or industrial design to chance. And we shouldn't leave collaboration to chance either. The new field of collaboration design seeks to create intentional experiences for teams to thrive. And anyone can practice collaboration design, not just professional facilitators.

We hope that you have enjoyed exploring—in this book and in your mind—the different components of deploying a comprehensive transformation of a collaboration culture.

Now it's time for action!

All of the stories we've shared ended up having a big impact—millions of dollars, thousands of happier people. The other thing they have in common is that they always start with one person. Just one person who empowered their teams to feel safe and creative to solve anything. One person who takes the lead and who becomes a role model.

Human disconnection is the biggest problem we have at work today. We believe we have a systematic approach for solving it: collaborative intelligence. But we need courageous people to step up. Change starts with making collaboration better one team at a time. Change starts with you.

 Learn more and meet like-minded people at **www.collaborativeintelligence.com**

Acknowledgments

Writing a book is a great example of team collaboration. It usually takes a fairly large group of people with diverse roles and inputs to put one together. This project was no exception. In fact, we'd go as far to say everyone working to make this book a reality was collaborating intelligently.

First, we'd like to thank our colleagues at Mural who provided input and reviewed text and images with us. Justin Owings really drove the project forward and accompanied us the entire way—from conception to completion—reading every word and providing thoughtful feedback. We also received feedback in various forms from Mark Tippin, Sunni Brown, Laïla von Alvensleben, Emilia Åström, Chris Pacione, Bill Lucas, Seema Jain, Dustin Stiver, Katie Bullard, Pete Maher, Steve Farrell, Erik Flowers, Steve Schofield, Paul Tomlinson, Helen Odom, Ray Savona, and Jen Standen.

Douglas Ferguson, Laurel Farrer, Joe Lalley, and others in our community provided invaluable external review.

We're also indebted to the talented team at XPLANE for designing the book and creating all of the wonderful artwork throughout: Nancy Sewell, Tim May, and Jeffery Frankenhauser.

A special thank you goes to the team at the Reading List for navigating the project and providing expert editorial support, in particular, Sal Borriello, who made it all happen.

We thank all of our partners who have engaged with us over the years in a broader conversation about collaboration and gave us the inspiration and confidence to move toward collaborative intelligence. To start, we're indebted to Al Ramadan, Jason Wellcome, Mike Bruno, and Ashli Walkiewicz at Play Bigger for setting us on this journey. But there are many others, including Fede Nahon from Arketify, Dave Gray and Sunni Brown from Gamestorming, and everyone in our Playmaker community.

And finally, we thank our customers, without whom this book would not have been possible. We've learned a lot together with you! We thank

Rob Dickins, Amy Bunszel, Melissa Schmidt, Eric Fain, and others at Autodesk; Doug Powell, Adam Cutler, Michael Ackerbauer, Katrina Alcorn, Lee Duncan, Sarah B .Nelson, and others at IBM; to Erik Flowers, Leslie Witt, Carvalho, Gerald, and Ariel Alvarez at Intuit; Rob Poel and Usam Shen from Steelcase; Thomas Weis, Fabian Leitz, and Ingo Widmann at SAP; Leticia Britos Cavagnaro, Janaki Kumar, and Sam Yen at the d.School; Pete Bellamy, Kelly Cooper, Ashley Becker, and others at EY; Tim Brown, Pontus Wahlgren and Joe Gerberds at IDEO...and the countless others from companies—such as Accenture, USAA, Spotify, Vanguard, Facebook, Allstate, Publicis Groupe, ThoughtWorks, Booz Allen Hamilton, Kyndryl—who have provided inspiration, encouragement, and support over the past decade.

About the Authors

Mariano Battan

Mariano Battan co-founded Mural, a collaborative intelligence company. He is a serial entrepreneur with an exit to Disney on his resume, an EY Entrepreneur of the Year 2021 Finalist, and an inventor by trade. He is passionate about connecting the next generation of knowledge workers to the development of their collaboration design skills, so they can ideate and solve hard problems together.

Previously, he co-founded Three Melons, a video game studio that designed and published online games for clients like LEGO, Disney, Mattel, and Warner Bros. Three Melons created more than 50 games as well as the soccer-based Facebook game Bola!, which had more than 20 million players globally in 2010. The company was acquired in 2010 by Playdom, then Disney, where Mariano served as creative director following the acquisition. He then co-founded Idea.me, a leading crowdfunding site for the Latin American region.

Mariano is an active angel investor and startup advisor at Endeavor.org, a global non-profit leading the high-impact entrepreneurship movement. As an Endeavor entrepreneur, he mentors other founders at various stages of their scaleup journey. He is a graduate of the Endeavor Leadership Program by the Stanford Graduate School of Business.

Jim Kalbach

Jim Kalbach is the chief evangelist at Mural and has been with the company since 2015. He is a noted author, speaker, and instructor in experience design, strategy, and visual methods, as well as remote facilitation. Jim's personal mission is to make imagination work possible in global organizations, anywhere, anytime. Early on, Jim was instrumental in growing several of Mural's largest customers, including IBM, SAP, Intuit, and more.

In 2018, Jim coauthored Mural's guide to remote meetings, *Facilitating Remote Workshops*. He is also the author of *Designing Web Navigation* (2016, O'Reilly); *Mapping Experiences* (2016, O'Reilly; 2nd Ed, 2020), focusing on the role of visualizations in strategy and innovation; and *The Jobs To Be Done Playbook* (2020, Rosenfeld Media), offering techniques organizations can follow to turn market insight into action. More recently, Jim co-founded the JTBD Toolkit, an online learning platform on the topic of jobs to be done (www.jtbdtoolkit.com).